YOUNG PHOTOGRAPHER'S POCKET BOOK

Designed and produced by Autumn Publishing Limited,
10 Eastgate Square, Chichester.

Editors: Ingrid Goldsmid
Rachael Jones

Typeset: CitySet Limited, Chichester

Photographs: Richard Crisp
Terry Pickering, Colour Precision Studios, Chichester
Autumn Publishing Limited

Illustrations: Jill Dickin

ISBN 0 361 06294 X

Published 1984 by Purnell Books, Paulton, Bristol, BS18 5LQ
A member of the BPCC Group.

Printed and bound in Great Britain by
Hazell Watson & Viney Limited,
Member of the BPCC Group,
Aylesbury, Bucks

YOUNG PHOTOGRAPHER'S POCKET BOOK

Jacqueline Dineen

Purnell

INTRODUCTION

To be a good photographer is by no means a matter of having a bigger, more expensive or more complex camera than anyone else. Excellent photographs can be taken using a simple camera with few controls. The secret is to be able to find pictures in the most ordinary and everyday situations and to capture them on film.

How to do this wherever you find yourself, how to compose a picture in the viewfinder, what to look for when taking a photograph, are all explained in a straightforward and simple way in this handbook.

This book also shows how different equipment can help you achieve success in different areas of photography, such as indoor work using flash, and action pictures. Technical information on cameras, lenses and other equipment is set out in an easy-to-read manner, and if you want to go further and develop your own photographs, then this too is explained in such a way as to take out all the mystery. Developing your own pictures can soon be as natural a process to you as taking them.

I hope that this book will enable you to enjoy your photography and help you become a proficient and enthusiastic photographer.

Jacqueline Dineen

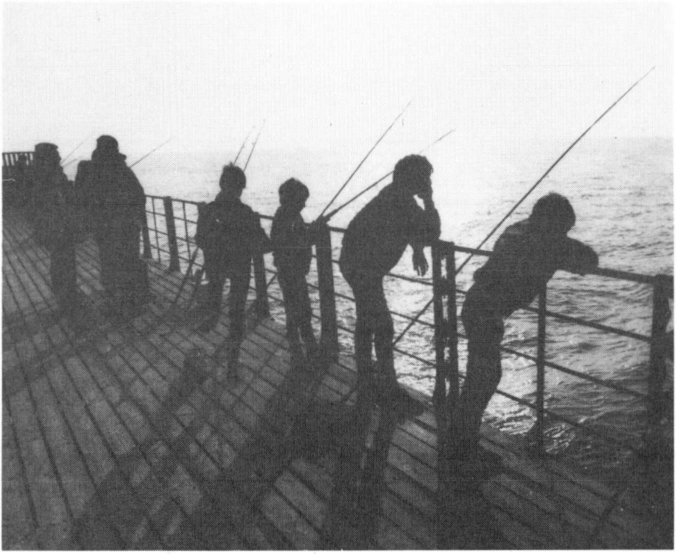

Contents

CHAPTER 1

How a Camera Works

All cameras, even the most complicated, work in the same way. They are boxes which let in a small amount of light through a hole to make an impression on film. It is very important that the amount of light is just right, and this is what most of the controls on a camera are for.

Light passes into the camera through the LENS. Lenses are specially cut pieces of glass which are shaped so that the IMAGE is sharp and accurate when it reaches the film.

Different cameras have different controls. Some cameras are simple, others are not, and we shall look at the various types in the next chapter. Basically, though, if your camera is a simple one with no controls, you don't have to worry too much, except to make sure that there is enough light to take a good picture. If your camera does have controls, you can take pictures even if there is very little light, if you adjust the controls carefully.

Look at your camera and read the instruction book that comes with it. Whatever type of camera it is, you will find some or all of the controls described in this chapter. (We are looking at a camera fitted with a standard 50mm lens – other lenses are discussed in chapter 4.)

The Viewfinder

The viewfinder, as the name suggests, is the small glass window you look through to see what your picture will show. Some cameras have DIRECT viewfinders, others have REFLEX viewfinders.

Simple cameras have direct viewfinders. This means that the lens and the viewfinder are separate. You look through the viewfinder and choose what you think is the perfect picture; but

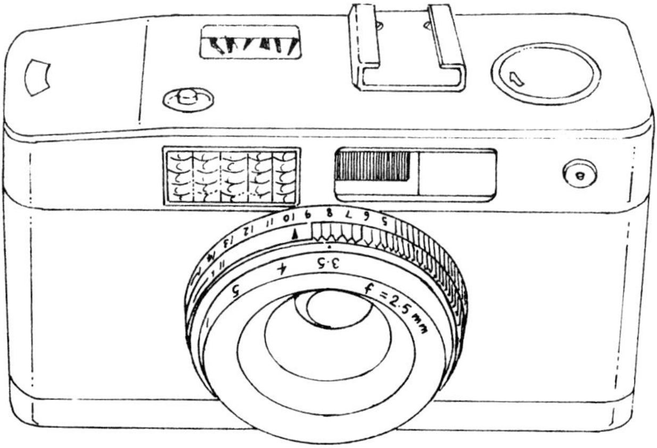

Camera fitted with standard 50mm lens

the lens sees the scene from a slightly different place and this changes the picture. The result is that things near the edge of the frame may be chopped off in the photograph (a mistake called PARALLAX ERROR). Many cameras have marks on the viewfinder to show how near the edge you can go. Close-up shots need to be even more accurate, and some viewfinders have extra marks to show the frame for a picture of something closer than 2 metres.

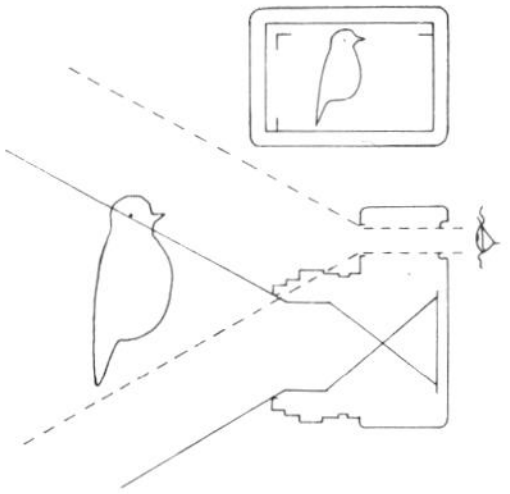

Direct viewfinder

This is not a problem with a reflex, or through-the-lens, viewfinder because the viewfinder and the lens see the same thing. The image passes through the lens to a mirror which reflects it up to the viewfinder, so the photographer knows exactly what will be in the picture.

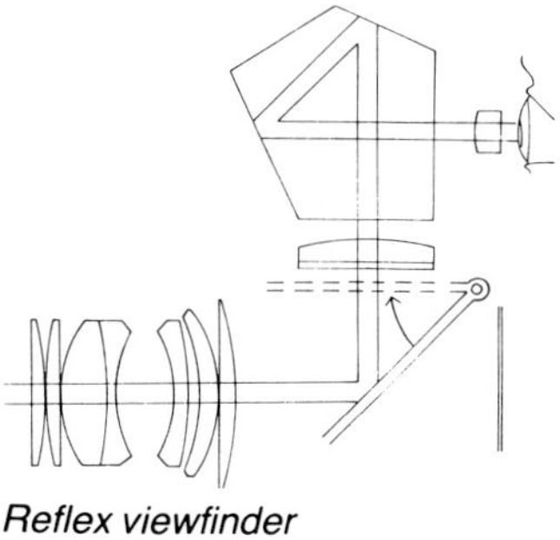

Reflex viewfinder

The Aperture

The aperture is the hole in the front of the camera, behind the

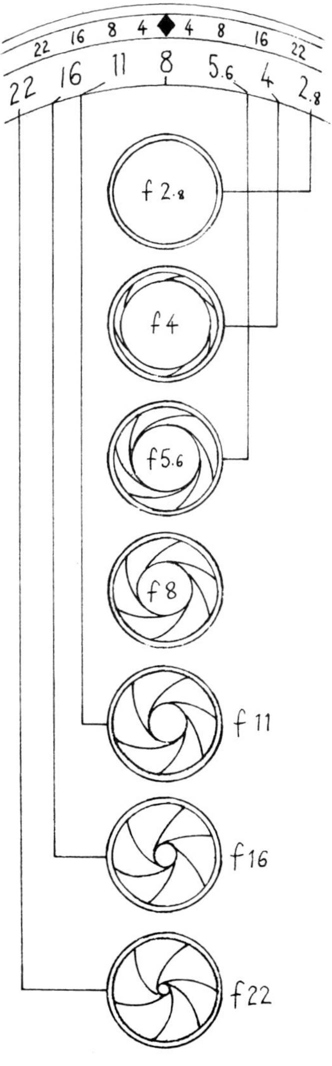

F-stops on aperture control

lens, which controls the amount of light entering the camera when a picture is taken. On an adjustable camera, this hole can be made smaller or larger by the photographer. You would need a large aperture on a cloudy day to make sure that enough light reached the film, but on a bright, sunny day you would use a small aperture to cut down the amount of light.

If you have a camera with an adjustable aperture, look at the aperture control now. You will see a row of figures, called F-NUMBERS or F-STOPS. These normally run from f/1.7 or f/2 up to f/16 or f/22. The smallest f-number, say f/1.7, is the largest aperture and lets in the most light. The largest f-number is the smallest aperture and lets in the least light.

Being able to control the aperture allows for two functions. One, of course, is to let more or less light into the camera, but the choice of aperture also changes the DEPTH OF FIELD. This is the amount of a scene, from front to back, which will be IN FOCUS (sharp) on the final picture. If you look at your camera again, you should see a depth of field indicator which shows two distances for every f-number. The area between these distances will be in focus at that f-number. Basically, the larger the aperture, the shorter the depth of field. So if you wanted to take a close-up of a flower with the background out of focus, you would open right up to f/2 or f/2.8 to let in plenty of light, and focus very carefully on the flower; the depth of field may be so small that some petals are in focus and

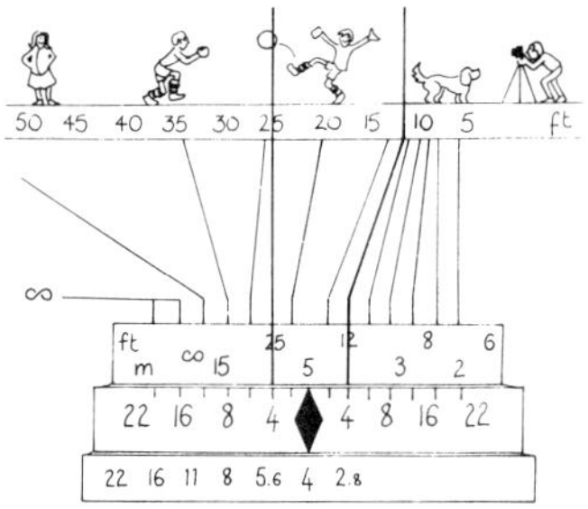

Aperture controls depth of field

others are not. If you wanted to take a scene with everything in focus as far as the eye can see, you would choose a small aperture, such as f/11 or f/16.

The Shutter

The shutter opens and closes when you press the shutter release button, and lets light into the camera through the aperture. When you choose an aperture because of the depth of field, you must also check whether the aperture will let the right amount of light into the camera. Suppose you want a picture with long depth of field, and you choose an aperture of f/11. Naturally, this will not let in as much light as an aperture of f/8 – only half as much, in fact. So how can you be sure that enough light reaches the film? The answer is to change the amount of time that the shutter is open.

The length of time the shutter is open is governed by the shutter speed. Shutter speeds are given in fractions of a second, or whole seconds for very slow ones. The range is from slow speeds of perhaps 2 or even 4 seconds, to very fast ones of 1/1000 or 1/2000 of a second. The slow speeds allow you to

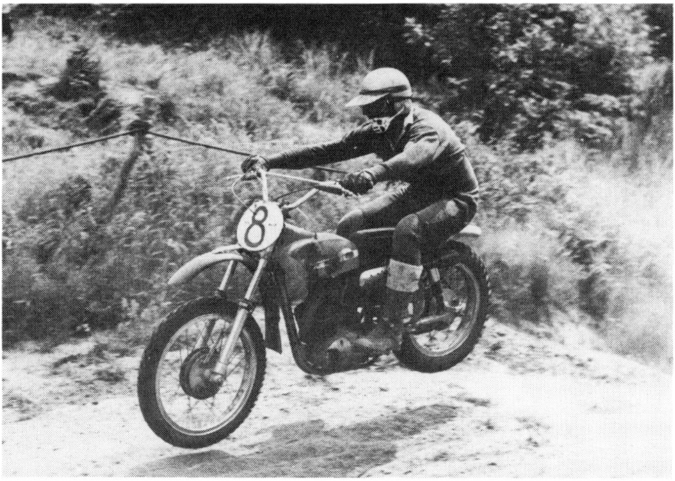

By using a fast shutter speed you can freeze movement

take pictures under very poor lighting conditions – at night or on a very dull day, or even indoors. With the fast speeds, you can freeze movement, and so take action shots.

The relationship between aperture and shutter speed is a very important one. If you have an adjustable camera, you will need a LIGHT METER (see page 13) to tell you which shutter speed to use with which aperture to give you the correct EXPOSURE for your picture (to let in the right amount of light). Every aperture setting is half the size of the one next to it (f/8 is half the size of f/5.6, f/11 is half the size of f/8, and so on), so you double the shutter speed each time to get the same picture. If you increase the size of the aperture by one f-stop, you halve the shutter speed. Suppose you choose a small aperture, such as f/11. Your light meter might show a shutter speed of 1/125. If f/11 is 1/125, the next aperture, f/8, which is twice as large, would only need the shutter open for half as long – 1/250. At f/16, on the other hand, you would need the shutter open for twice as long, or 1/60 of a second.

Problems can arise in dull weather or when you are taking action shots. In dull weather, you may still want long depth of field, but find that at f/11 you only get a reading of, say 1/30 of a second. Anything slower than 1/60 is tricky because the chances are that you will shake the camera slightly as you press the shutter release, and the result will be a blurred photograph. So for a hand-held shot on a dull day, you might have to use an aperture of f/8 and a shutter speed of 1/60, and give up some depth of field (not have quite as much of the scene in focus as you would really like).

Action shots are difficult if the light is not very good, because they need a fast shutter speed. A fast shutter speed needs a large aperture, so once again the depth of field may not be as great as you would like it to be. In poor light you may not be able to get a small enough aperture combined with a fast shutter speed to give you the picture you want.

For example, if you want to take a picture of a car travelling fairly fast, you will need a speed of at least 1/500 to 'freeze' the movement. On this particular day the smallest aperture you could use with this speed might be f/4, which wouldn't give you much depth of field, so you might have to change the composition you had in mind. In other words, you may not have quite so much choice over the sort of picture you can take if you are tied to a fast shutter speed under certain conditions. (In fact, films do come in different speeds to cope with different lighting conditions, and we shall look at this in chapter 3.)

As a quick guide to exposure (the relationship between the aperture and shutter), here is a possible range of combinations your light meter might show you for the same picture.

Aperture	*Shutter speed*
f/22	1/30
– too slow for a hand-held picture	
f/16	1/60
f/11	1/125
f/8	1/250
f/5.6	1/500
– good exposures for general photography	
f/4	1/1000
f/2.8	1/2000
– not much depth of field	

Focusing

The third control you need to know about on an adjustable camera is the focus control. On a simple camera, the focus control is set at a distance which is suitable for most general photography (aperture and shutter speed are also fixed to give long depth of field). If you have a focus control on your camera, you can change the focus to get a clear image for close-ups as well as distant objects.

Look at your camera again. You will be able to see, at one end of the focusing or distance scale, the symbol ∞ which means INFINITY. This is for objects as far away as the eye can see. At the other end is the closest distance at which you can focus and still get a clear image – maybe half a metre. Pictures taken closer than this will be blurred. In between, marked in metres, or feet and metres, is a range of distances.

With some cameras, you have to work out how far away the object is and set the focus control accordingly. Other cameras have through-the-lens focusing. You look through the viewfinder and twist the focusing ring until the scene you are photographing

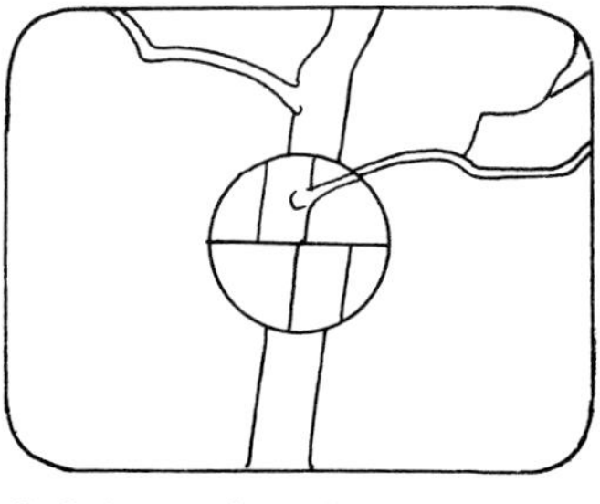

Split-image focusing

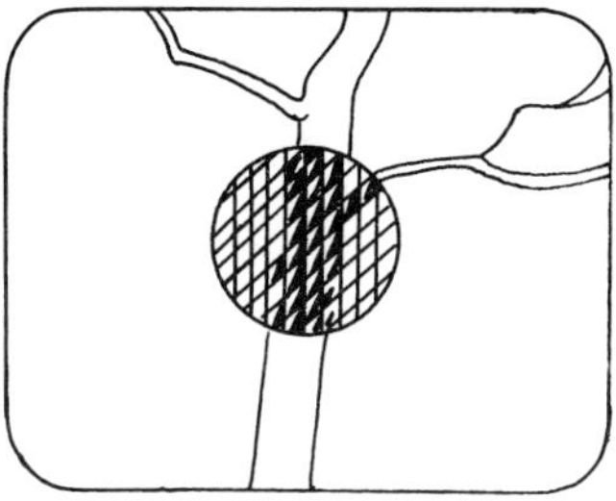

Microprism focusing

looks sharp. Some cameras have SPLIT-IMAGE focusing. A small area in the centre of the viewfinder shows a split image until it is focused correctly, when the two halves come together. A similar idea is a small fuzzy area in the centre which becomes clear when correctly focused. This is called MICROPRISM focusing. RANGEFINDER focusing uses a double image. You focus by twisting the focusing ring until you get a single image.

If you look at the depth of field scale again, you will see that focusing is far more important for larger apertures, such as f/2.8, where the depth of field is very short. At, say, f/11 you would be in focus from 3 metres away to infinity; at f/2.8 you have to focus very carefully to get a single object perfectly sharp.

Before going any further, it is as well to practise using these controls and thinking about their relationship to each other. They are all linked by the depth of field that is needed and the relationship between aperture and shutter speed. Study your own camera, and if it has a focusing ring, practise focusing on objects at different distances and getting them pin sharp. Look at the focusing scale and see how far away different objects are and what the depth of field would be for various apertures. This is the best way of becoming familiar with the three controls and how they work.

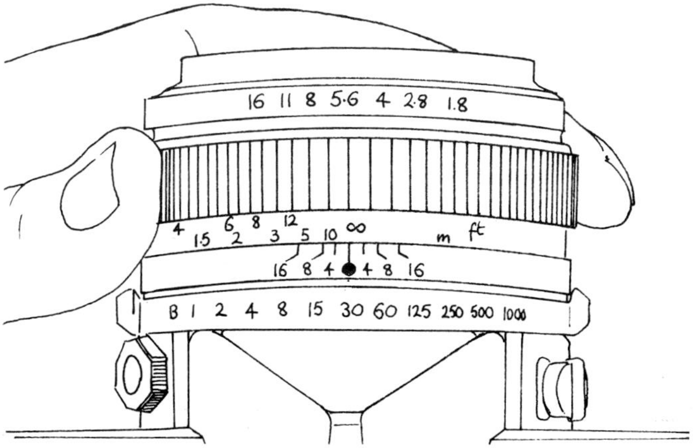

Light meter in viewfinder

Exposure (Light) Meters

As you become used to taking pictures, you may be able to judge what aperture and shutter speed combinations you need for certain light conditions. The guide that comes with a film is helpful, too. Even so, it is not possible to be really accurate by guesswork, and this is why photographers use exposure (light) meters to help them work out what settings to use.

Bright and cloudy adjustment

Hand-held light meter

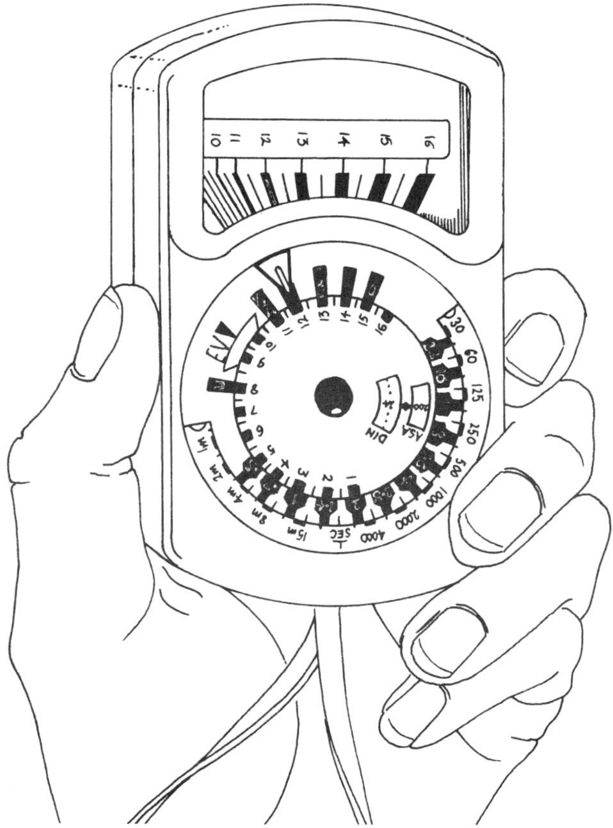

The simplest type of metering is the bright and cloudy adjustment found on some 110 cameras. This gives you two choices. A more complex (complicated) camera and light meter, of course, give you many more.

An exposure meter may be built into your camera, or you may use a separate hand-held meter. Nowadays, many cameras have a built-in light meter, and this makes life easier because there is one less thing to carry around.

A separate light meter has a moving needle which gives a LIGHT READING when you point the meter at the thing to be photographed. First set the film speed (see page 23) on the meter, and then take a reading. Set this reading on the dial, and it will give the range of aperture and shutter speed combinations you can use for that picture. If you are photographing a general scene, take the reading from the place where you plan to take the picture. If you want to get the correct exposure for one particular object, hold the meter close to that object to take a reading. When you point the meter in the general direction of a scene, it may include more sky in the reading than you plan for the picture. Because the sky is the brightest part, it may therefore give readings which make the rest of the scene come out UNDER-EXPOSED (too dark). To overcome this, partly shade the top of the meter, above the light cell, with your hand to cut out some of the sky. This will give a more accurate reading.

Some cameras have through-the-lens metering, which is easier to use because the light measured is for the actual scene you can see in the viewfinder. On some cameras the metering is shown in the viewfinder. On MANUAL cameras, you select both shutter speed and aperture, but on SEMI-AUTOMATIC cameras you choose one of these and the camera matches it with the correct partner. For example, on a camera with APERTURE PRIORITY, the

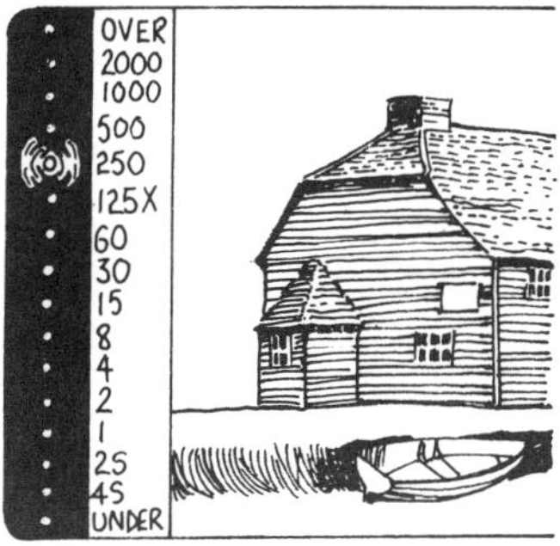

A light shows shutter speed

scale in the viewfinder shows shutter speeds only. You select the aperture you want to use, look at the scene through the viewfinder and press the light meter button, and a light appears next to the most appropriate shutter speed on the light meter. This is the speed the camera will use. If you want, say, a faster speed, you have to set a different aperture until the meter is showing the speed you want. Some semi-automatic cameras have SHUTTER PRIORITY, which works the other way round and is particularly useful for people who take a lot of action shots where the choice of shutter speed is all-important.

Sometimes the meter will show that the f-number you have chosen will give an OVER-EXPOSED shot (it can't choose a fast enough speed to stop too much light entering the camera). An over-exposed picture (too much light) has weak, washed-out colours.

There may not be enough light to give a reading for your aperture, and the meter will show 'under-exposed'. Sometimes – for example, if you are taking a picture with a bright sky and a dark subject – parts of the picture may come out under or over-exposed while others are all right. This is because the scene has too much CONTRAST (differences in light that are too great) for the meter to give a general reading. In this situation you have to choose what part of the picture to take a reading from so that you get the best overall result. (We shall look at this in more detail in later chapters.)

Some cameras are semi-automatic but can be switched to manual. This means that you have a wider choice of settings because you set both controls. Manual controls are useful if you have to choose a part of the scene to take a reading from, or if you want to try different settings for the same picture, to see which works best.

Completely AUTOMATIC cameras, of course, don't give the photographer any choice at all, but simply make a general setting for the scene being photographed.

In the next chapter we shall look at the different types of camera, and what each type will do.

Other Controls

You will probably be able to identify the other controls on your camera from the instructions that come with it. They are all quite straightforward.

FILM ADVANCE AND FRAME COUNTER

When you have taken a picture, you wind the film on with the film advance lever, ready for the next shot. The number of frames (pictures) you have taken appears on the frame counter so that you can keep a check. Many cameras will not take another picture if you have forgotten to wind on. This is a safety mechanism to prevent double exposures (two pictures on the same frame).

SHUTTER RELEASE

This is the button you press to take a photograph. Practise pressing it down smoothly so the camera doesn't shake.

FILM REWIND LEVER

When you have finished a film, you use the film rewind lever to wind it back into the cassette before you open the camera.

FILM SPEED DIAL

If your camera has a dial, it is important to set the correct speed of the film you are using before you take any pictures. (Film speeds are explained in chapter 3.)

FLASH SHOE

Flash gives extra light when it is needed. The flash gun, or flash cube, fits on to the flash shoe. Your camera may also have a special shutter speed setting, normally marked with an X, to use with flash.

These are the basic controls. Your camera may have more – or less. Study it carefully so that you know what all the controls are, and practise using the camera without a film in it until you feel completely comfortable. Practise setting exposures until you feel familiar with the different combinations you may get. Choose a general scene and take a light meter reading, noticing all the different combinations you could have for the same scene. Each of these combinations will give you a correctly exposed picture. Take a reading for a close-up, when you want to put the background out of focus. Remember that you need a large aperture to do this. What effect does this have on the shutter speed? Now try a reading which will give you the longest depth of field without making the shutter speed too slow. (Choose a bright scene for this, and then try the same thing on a cloudy day.) Imagine you want to take an action shot with a shutter speed of 1/500 and take a reading from, say, moving traffic – what aperture must you use to get this shutter speed?

The only way to become really familiar with exposure settings is to practise under all the conditions you can think of. Then you will have less chance of taking a wrongly exposed shot when it is a picture that really matters.

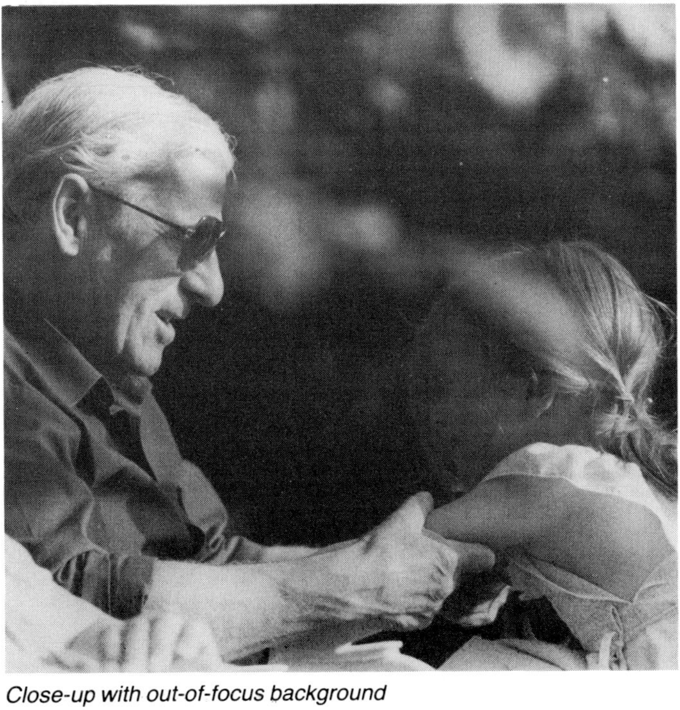

Close-up with out-of-focus background

CHAPTER 2

Choosing a Camera

If you haven't bought a camera yet, you may be feeling bewildered by the choice available. Which one should you get? What are the advantages and disadvantages of the different types, and which one will suit you best?

One important thing to consider is the cost. Cameras can be very expensive, and it may seem, as you look around a photographic shop, that this hobby is out of your reach – but prices cover a wide range and some cameras are very cheap, so don't be depressed if you can't afford the camera of your dreams staight away. Perhaps you will be able to buy one in the future, if you want to carry on and progress with your photography. In the meantime, there is bound to be a camera you can afford, which will give you plenty of enjoyment, and most pictures depend on the photographer seeing the chance of a good shot rather than on the equipment.

Good cameras can sometimes be bought second-hand. People often sell a camera because they want to move on to a new model, even though the camera is in excellent condition, so have a good look round before you make any decisions.

Cameras range from the simple, press-a-button type to the complex ones with all sorts of different controls. Broadly, they come into the following groups.

110 and 126 Cartridge-Loading Cameras

These are the simplest and cheapest cameras. They are easy to carry around as they fit into a pocket or bag, the film cartridges are easy to put in and there are very few controls to worry about; in fact, some have no controls at all. Others have simple focusing and exposure controls. There may be three positions for focusing, for portraits, groups or distant shots; and two different exposure settings, for sunny or cloudy weather.

You can take good general

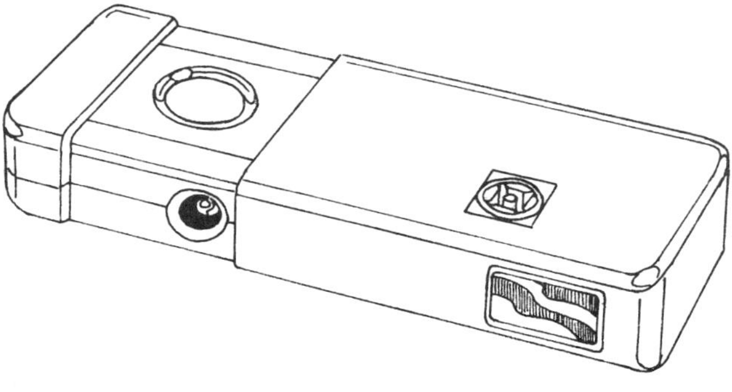

110 camera

pictures with a pocket camera of this sort, though the small negatives produced from a cartridge film mean that large prints cannot be made without losing quality. Other disadvantages are that because the shutter and aperture are fixed to a general setting and you can't alter the focus for close-ups, you are a bit more limited in the subjects you can take. Action shots are tricky, and fast-moving subjects are not possible. The lens does not focus any closer than about 1 metre, so you can't get in really close for subjects like flowers. And you can't take good pictures in poor light conditions unless you use flash.

Having said all that, there is plenty you *can* do with a pocket camera, so it is only if you want to specialise in close-up or action photography that you should rule out the possibility of getting one. If you already have a 110 or 126, don't feel that you have to rush off and buy a new camera before reading on. Most pictures can be taken very satisfactorily with a simple camera.

110 and 126 cameras either take flash cubes or have a built-in flash gun. The viewfinder is the direct type so there will be parallax error unless you frame your pictures carefully, but there is often a frame marked in the viewfinder to avoid this. These cameras are particularly useful for quick photographs, such as at parties, because you don't have to worry about choosing suitable speeds and settings.

Disc Cameras

The disc camera is a fairly new type of automatic camera. The film comes in a lightweight disc rather than a roll. The camera itself is slim and flat, and fits into a pocket or bag. This camera offers more scope than a 110, although there are often no manual controls. There is an automatic exposure control, and built-in flash which works automatically if the lighting is too low for the camera's exposure range. The camera has an f/2.8 lens with fixed focus between 1.3 metres and infinity; some models also have a close-up setting,

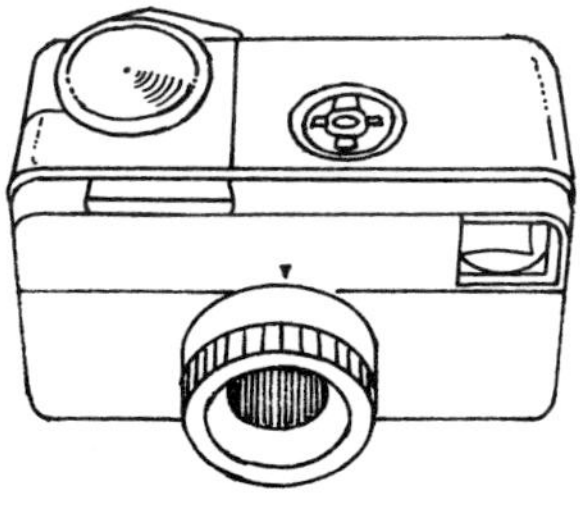

126 camera

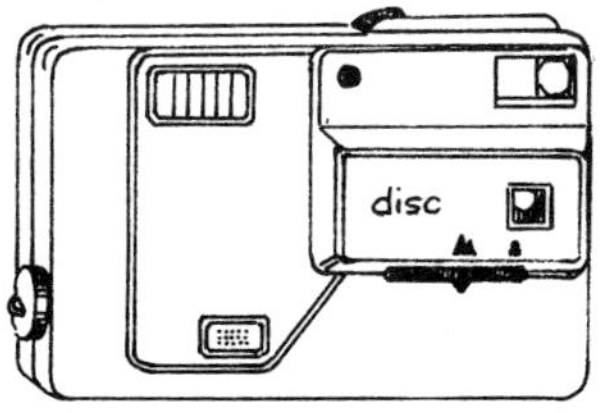

Disc camera

with parallax correction (to avoid cutting off parts of the subject), which is in focus from half a metre to 1.3 metres.

Advantages of this camera are that it is extremely simple to use – the photographer does not even have to remember to wind the film on as the camera does this automatically too. It is also very neat and light to carry around, and can take a wider range of pictures than a 110 or 126. Disadvantages for the keen photographer are that you have no choice at all over what you do apart from framing the picture, and that it is not particularly cheap. You could get a camera with more flexibility for the same sort of price. It all depends on what you want from your camera.

35mm Non-Reflex Camera

All 35mm cameras are named after the type of film they use, which is 35 millimetres wide and comes in cassettes. 35mm film gives larger negatives than cartridge film, which means better quality prints that can be blown up to large sizes. This type of camera is a good all-rounder which need not be expensive, and you can often find fairly cheap second-hand ones. The range of 35mm non-reflex cameras available is very large, and you really need to have a good look in a photographic shop and compare the different models. They can be manual or automatic, and the amount of control you have over exposure varies a lot. Some have simple symbol settings, others have a full range of f-numbers and shutter speeds. Some have rangefinder focusing and a built-in light meter. Ask whether the camera takes any ACCESSORIES (extra gadgets), such as FILTERS (see chapter 4), and whether it has built-in flash.

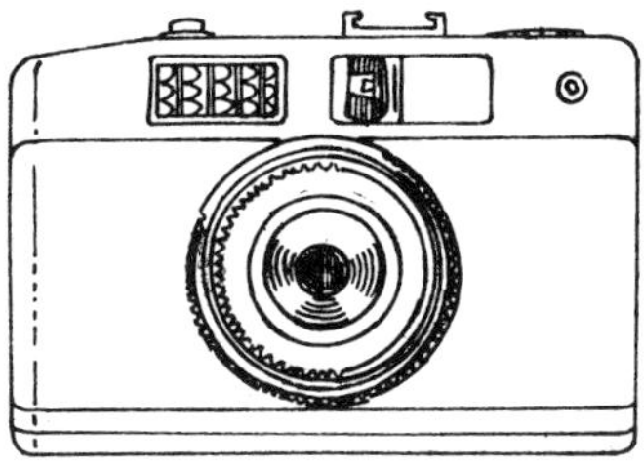

35mm non-reflex camera

Advantages of the 35mm non-reflex camera are that it is normally light and easy to carry around, particularly the compact version; it allows for more flexibility than a 110 or a 126 camera, and it need not cost the earth. There are plenty of different types, of varying complexity and price, to choose from.

A disadvantage, however, is that 35mm non-reflex cameras are fixed-lens, which means that you cannot change to a telephoto or any other lens, but have to use the standard lens provided with the camera. The viewfinder is direct vision rather than through-the-lens, though most have a frame to avoid parallax error.

35mm Single-Lens Reflex (SLR) Camera

This is the most popular type of camera for the keen photographer because it offers the most scope of all. The lens can be changed for a telephoto, a wide-angle or a close-up lens (see chapter 4). The through-the-lens viewfinder and focusing screen make framing and focusing a picture more or less trouble-free. SLRs have a full range of apertures and shutter speeds, and can be focused for close-ups.

Most SLR cameras have built-in light meters, and they can be fully automatic, semi-automatic, manual, or a combination of automatic and manual, which means that you can switch from one to the other depending on the type of picture you want to take. If you decide on an SLR, think carefully about how automatic you want it to be. You may like the idea of getting the results without having to worry about setting the controls. But you are limited if you want to try exposures which the camera doesn't agree with, or if you are taking pictures in difficult conditions which the automatic camera won't allow for. Cameras which give a choice of automatic or manual use are popular for this reason, but they are more expensive.

Second-hand SLR cameras

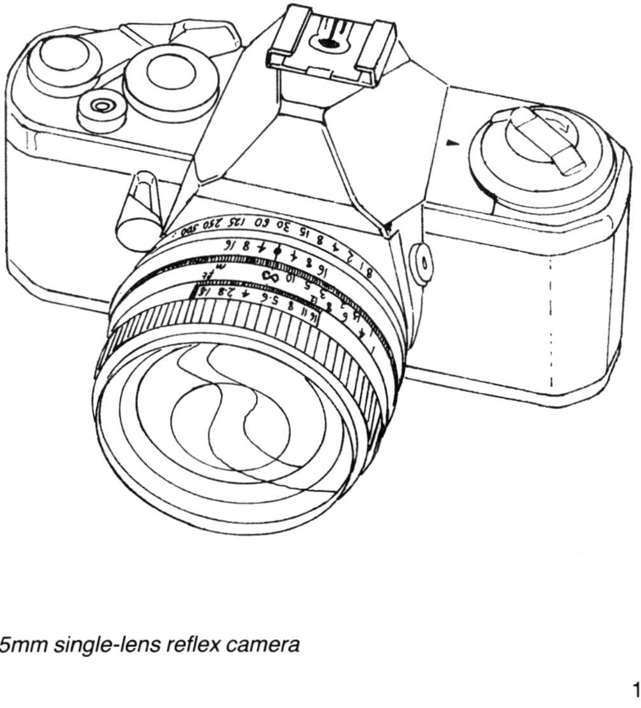

35mm single-lens reflex camera

are often manual only, and are heavier than the modern ones. They may not have built-in light meters or focusing screens, and there may be problems with getting lenses to fit them. So look very carefully at a second-hand camera and ask as many questions as you can about it before buying.

The disadvantages of the SLR are its size and weight, for the photographer who wants a camera he can slip in his pocket. Though they are lighter and more compact than they used to be, these cameras still have bulky lenses and need to be carried on the shoulder or round the neck. If you have a gadget bag full of accessories as well, you can find that you are walking round draped like a Christmas tree in order to take a few simple shots. But SLR cameras can be the most versatile, and produce good results in all kinds of conditions.

Twin-lens reflex camera

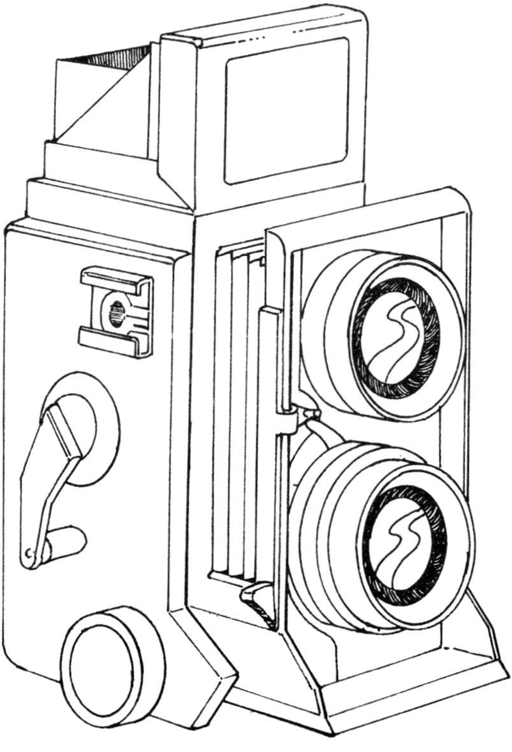

120 Twin-Lens Reflex (TLR) Camera

This camera is mentioned here because you can sometimes buy a second-hand TLR for a reasonable price. The 120 roll film which this camera takes produces large square negatives, and is popular with photographers who like plenty of detail in their pictures.

A twin-lens reflex has two identical lenses, one above the other. The lower lens takes the picture and the other is the viewfinder. The camera is not held up to the eye, though. The photographer holds the camera at about waist height and looks down on the viewing screen. As with SLR viewfinders, the image passes through the lens to a mirror which reflects it up to the viewing screen. Because there are two lenses, there can be problems with parallax error.

TLR cameras normally have a full range of exposure settings and can be focused accurately. Some of them will take other lenses, but of course you have to buy two lenses every time!

Instant Picture Camera

These cameras use special paper rather than film. Each frame is pushed out by the camera after the shot is taken and the print develops as you wait. There are cheap, simple instant cameras or more complex models with aperture and shutter controls, flash and other variations. The advantage of this type of camera is that the picture is printed straight away, and so you can compare it with the subject and take another shot if necessary. One disadvantage is the size and bulkiness of the camera. Another is that the film packs are expensive, and there is no negative, so you can't make extra prints.

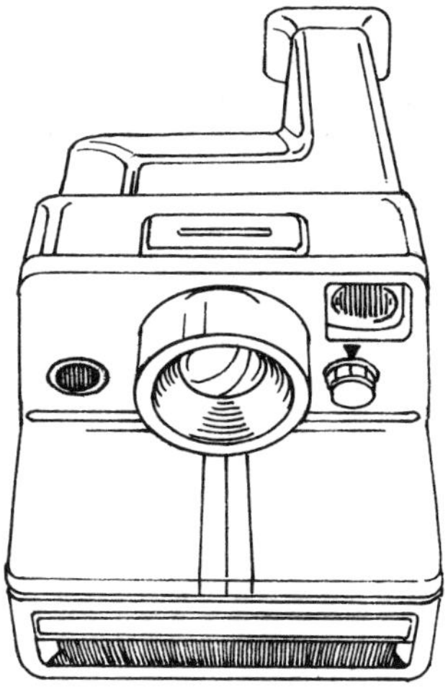

Instant picture camera

Which Camera?

How do you choose the most suitable camera? The best way to start is to think carefully about the sort of photography you want to do. If you are a beginner, you probably want to practise all sorts of different things before you decide whether to concentrate on one particular subject. For this you need a general camera, but you may not want to spend too much money until you know whether photography is really going to be your hobby. How much can you afford? Do you really want different lenses and gadgets, or will you be using a standard lens most of the time?

How important is it to have a light camera that is easy to carry around? Do you want a manual or an automatic camera? Are you keen on the idea of close-ups, or action shots? Do you want a built-in light meter and flash, or are you prepared to carry separate attachments around with you?

Go along to a good camera shop and have a discussion with the dealer about the different types of camera he has in stock, and what they do. Don't be afraid to ask questions. If you are buying a second-hand camera from a camera shop, make sure there is some form of guarantee, in case the camera doesn't work as well as it should. If you buy from a friend, ask if you can try the camera first or see some recent pictures taken with it.

The outlines in this book give you some idea of what the different cameras do, and therefore what questions to ask about specific models. There are many variations, and new cameras are coming out all the time, so make a careful study and read camera magazines before you decide. If you become a keen photographer, your camera will be your constant companion, so it is important to get one you like.

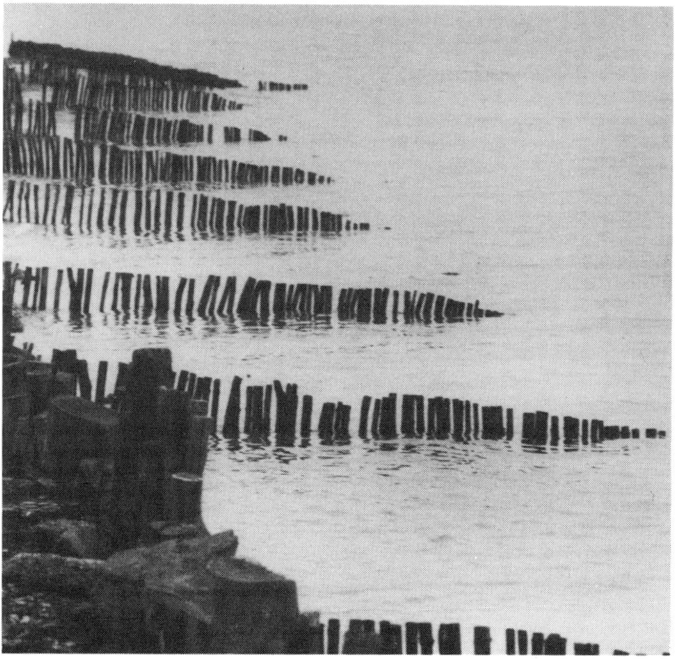

Pattern picture

CHAPTER 3

Choosing a Film

So now you have bought a camera and of course you want to try it out. You need a film for it. Buying a film is not quite the simple matter of going into a shop and saying, 'Can I have a film, please?'. You have to decide first between black and white and colour, and between colour prints and colour slides. Then you have to know what film speed you want. It is worth knowing something about the different films available, because you will get better results if you use the correct film for the job.

What is Film?

A film is a strip of plastic, coated with an emulsion which is very sensitive to light. As soon as light touches the film, it leaves an image. This is why it is so important that no light gets to the film before you mean it to. If the back of your camera flies open with a film in it, the film, or part of it, will be ruined because the light will have got to it.

The films used with 110 and 126 cameras are protected in light-tight cartridges. 35mm film comes in a light-tight cassette. The film comes out of the cassette inside the camera when an exposure is made and the film is wound on for the next shot; and you wind it back into the cassette after the last picture.

The length of the film inside the container varies. There may be enough for 12, 20, 24 or 36 exposures. There are different films for black and white prints, colour prints and colour slides.

Film Speeds

When you buy a film, you will see that it has an ASA NUMBER on it. The term ASA (American Standards Association) is used to describe the film speed. Your camera may have a film speed dial giving a range of ASA numbers, so that you can set the correct speed each time you load a new film into the camera. You must set the speed on a camera with a built-in light meter in order to get an accurate reading. The same applies to a hand-held meter. So, every time you load a new film, remember to set the film speed. Even if it doesn't affect the camera's metering, it will remind you which film you are using.

Different films are coated with slightly different light-sensitive chemicals which affect the way the film reacts to light. The speed indicates how light-sensitive that particular film is. The faster the film, the more sensitive it is to light. Therefore, fast films need a shorter exposure than slow films, so can be used in dim light conditions or when a fast shutter speed is needed.

If you look closely at photographs, particularly ENLARGEMENTS (large prints), you can sometimes see that they are made up of tiny dots. This is called the GRAIN of the film. Fast films are more grainy than slow ones, which means that the tiny dots are more noticeable, especially when pictures are enlarged. So slower films are more suitable if good-quality enlargements are wanted, or for clear detail.

Film speeds run from 25 ASA up to 1000 ASA, and they are similar for colour and black and white. The rule to remember is the lower the number, the slower the film – 25 ASA is the slowest and 1000 ASA the fastest available at the moment.

The reason that film is made in a range of speeds is so that good pictures can be taken in all kinds of lighting conditions. Even the seasons of the year alter things. Your camera may be loaded with a medium-speed film, such as 100 ASA, for the summer, but when winter comes, you will get completely different light readings because the winter light is much weaker. Sometimes you may not get a reading at all for the picture you want. For winter photography, therefore, a faster film such as 400 ASA would be more suitable.

SLOW FILMS (25–65 ASA)
Slow films produce high quality pictures with plenty of detail, and

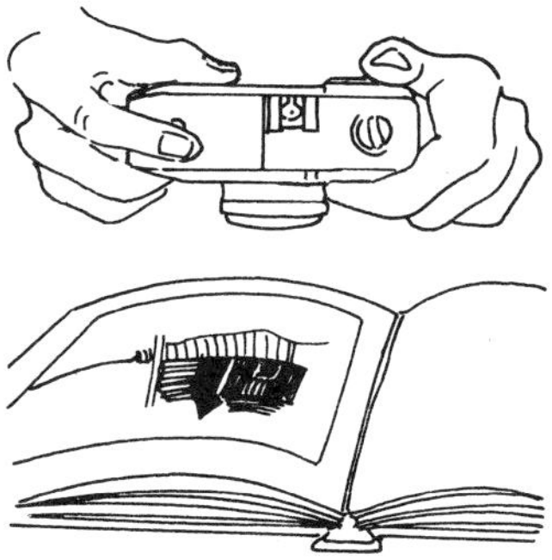

Using 25–65 ASA film

are good for static (still) subjects, particularly if you want to make enlargements. However, unless the light is bright, they have to be used with a large aperture which reduces the depth of field, or with a slow shutter speed which gives problems with movement.

MEDIUM FILMS (100–200 ASA)
This is the usual type of film for general photography. The most commonly used speeds are 100

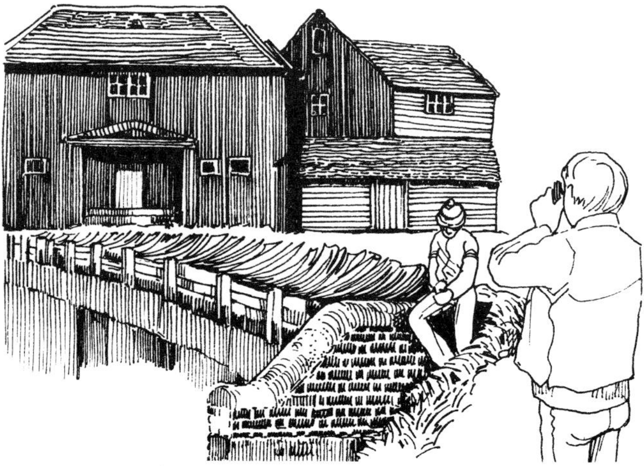

Using 100–200 ASA film

ASA for colour prints, and 125 ASA for black and white prints. 200 ASA is faster and so is useful when you need a bit more flexibility under varied lighting conditions. For example, daylight in autumn can vary from bright to very dull.

Medium film gives good results under normal conditions, allowing for action shots and close-ups, and giving a range of readings even on a cloudy day. If you are taking pictures of lots of different subjects, choose a medium-speed film unless lighting conditions are generally very poor. Enlargements will still be good, though without the fine detail of the fast films.

FAST FILMS (400–1000 ASA)

The most usual fast film for the general user is 400 ASA. This allows for fast shutter speeds, even in dull weather, which is useful for action photography. It also gives the photographer more choice of exposure settings in poor light conditions, such as winter light or late in the day. Usually prints from 400 ASA film cannot be BLOWN UP much (made much larger) without getting grainy.

The very fast 1000 ASA film is suitable for taking pictures when there is very little light and you don't want to use flash or artificial light.

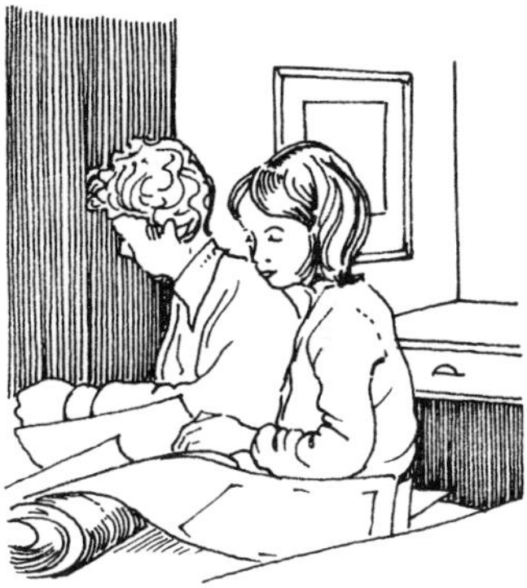

Use 1000 ASA film in dull conditions

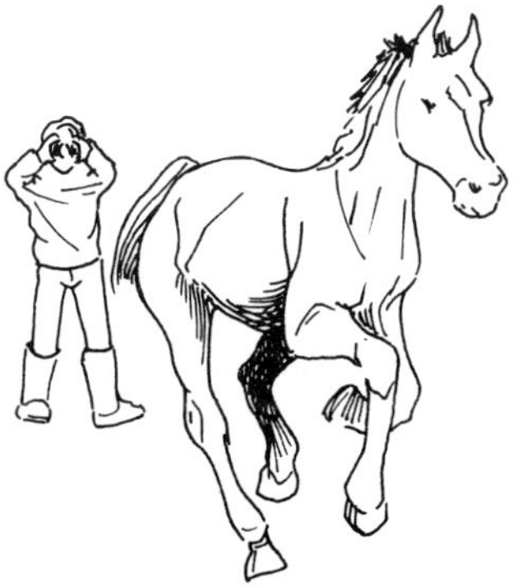

Use 400–1000 ASA film for action photography

Film speeds can be a confusing subject and many people stick to one or two favourite speeds for all their photography. If you have a 110 or 126 camera which takes cartridge film, you won't have much choice, as this film only comes in 100 ASA and 400 ASA for colour and 125 ASA for black and white. Disc film is always 200 ASA. 35mm cassette films have a larger range, but the same speeds are popular for general photography: for colour prints, 100 ASA most of the time, 200 ASA if this becomes a bit restricted, and 400 ASA for poor lighting conditions; for black and white, 125 ASA or 400 ASA. 64 ASA and 400 ASA are the most commonly used films for colour slides.

One other point to bear in mind when using colour film is that it is made for use in daylight or with flash. If you use it in artificial light, such as the electric lights of a room, without flash, the picture will have an overall orange tint. Special film is made for use with artificial light, or you could use a filter.

How Film Speed Affects Exposure

When you buy a film, you will find a list of suitable exposure combinations supplied with it. This is a useful guide and you should read it carefully.

You can get an idea of the different film speeds by comparing sets of exposures, for the same subject on the same day. Try this with your own camera or light meter. Choose a subject you would like to photograph. Set up a slow ASA, then a medium one and then a fast one. Take readings for each setting and compare the results. Try this with various subjects and judge which film speed would be the most suitable for your needs. (Remember that you have to use the whole film before you can change to a different speed!)

Look at the table below.

The following readings were taken of a general scene with some sun

Slow film (25 ASA)		Medium film (100 ASA)		Fast film (400 ASA)	
Aperture	*Shutter*	*Aperture*	*Shutter*	*Aperture*	*Shutter*
f/22	1/8	f/22	1/30	f/22	1/25
f/16	1/16	f/16	1/60	f/16	1/250
f/11	1/30	f/11	1/125	f/11	1/500
f/8	1/60	f/8	1/250	f/8	1/1000
f/5.6	1/125	f/5.6	1/500	f/5.6	1/2000
f/4	1/250	f/4	1/1000		
f/2.8	1/500	f/2.8	1/2000		

Colour slides (64 ASA)	
Aperture	*Shutter*
f/22	1/15
f/16	1/30
f/11	1/60
f/8	1/125
f/5.6	1/250
f/4	1/500
f/2.8	1/1000

You can see that 100 ASA gives the most scope for general photography. Only on f/22 was the reading too slow for a hand-held shot and even the largest aperture produced a reading. 64 ASA is only slightly slower – one stop difference each time – but with 25 ASA anything but a static subject would need a large aperture, and the range of hand-held shots starts at f/8. 400 ASA was too fast for the larger apertures under these conditions.

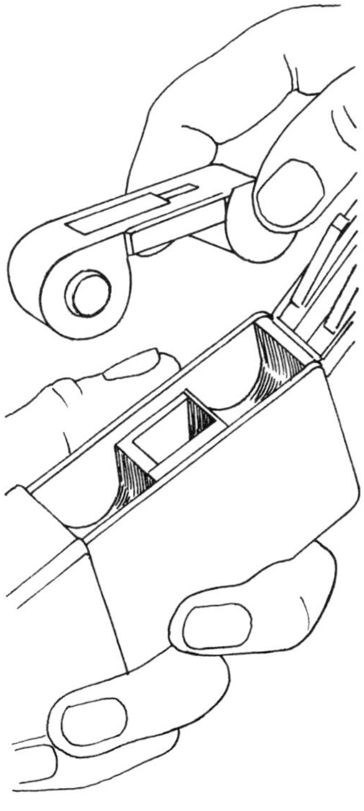

Open the back of the camera and drop in the cartridge

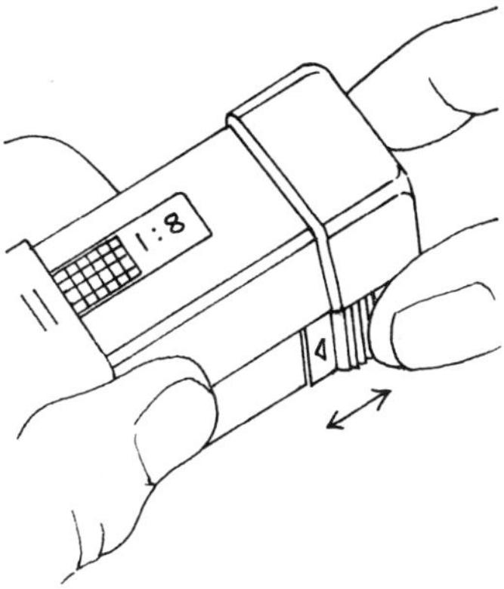

Wind on the film until the number 1 appears

Loading and Unloading Film

CARTRIDGE FILM

This is completely enclosed in a plastic case. Even so, it is best to load out of the sun. All you need to do is to open the back of the camera and drop the film in, making sure it is the right way round. Close the camera and press the shutter button, or wind on until the figure 1 appears in the frame counter. The film is now ready for your first picture.

When you have finished the film, wind on until it will go no further. Open the camera and take the film out.

CASSETTE FILM

This is not completely enclosed, so you have to be more careful when loading, because you need to pull some of the film out of the cassette to attach it to the spool in the camera. Always load in the shade or you might spoil the film.

Look at the instructions for your own camera. Open the

camera back. You will see an empty chamber on the left, below the rewind lever. Pull out the rewind lever and drop the cassette into this space, with the end of the film pointing towards the right. Push the rewind lever

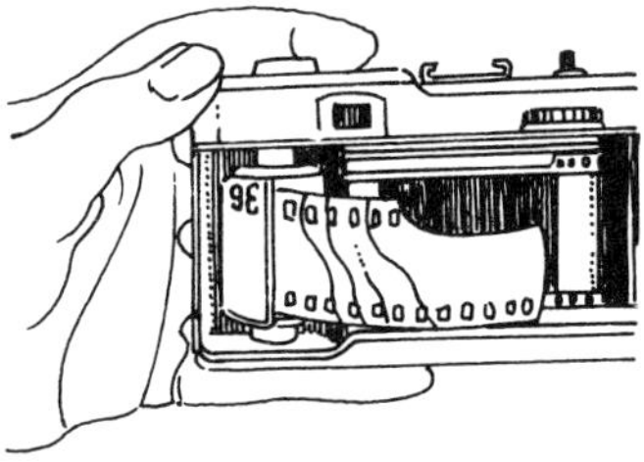

1 Pull out end of film

in to lock the film in place. Pull on the end of the film until you have enough to thread it on to the right-hand spool. Check with the instructions to see how the spool on your particular camera should

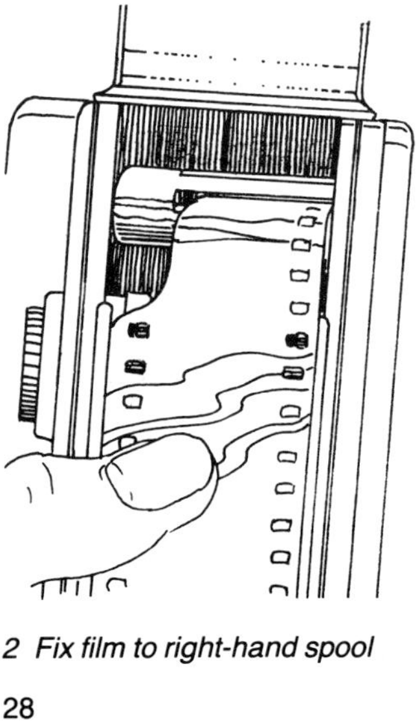

2 Fix film to right-hand spool

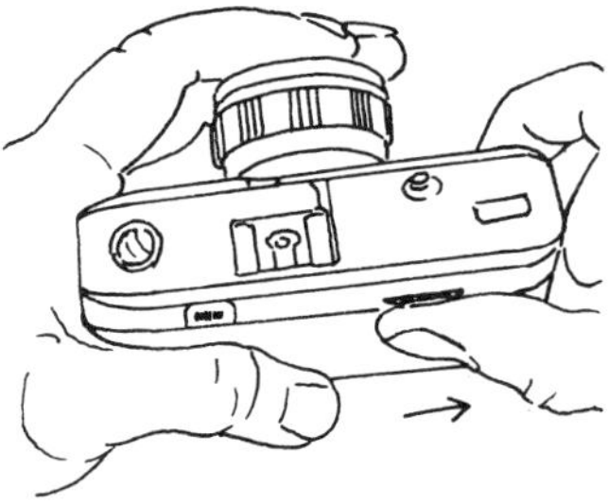

3 Close camera, wind film on

be threaded. Wind the film on a little, making sure that it is properly attached to the top and bottom sprockets and cannot slip off the spool. Close the camera back, press the shutter release and wind on until the figure 1 appears on the frame counter. This normally takes two or three exposures and is necessary to get rid of the early part of the film which has been exposed to the light. Set the film speed dial. The camera is now ready for your first picture.

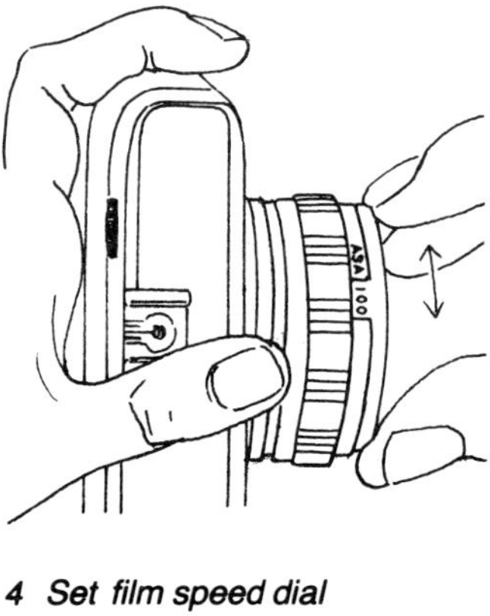

4 Set film speed dial

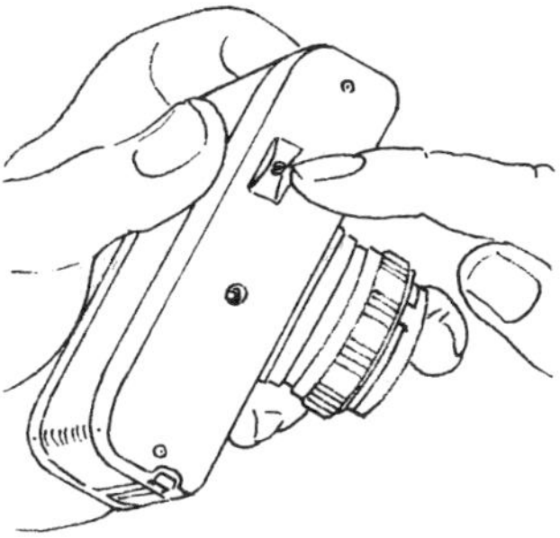

Press in the rewind button

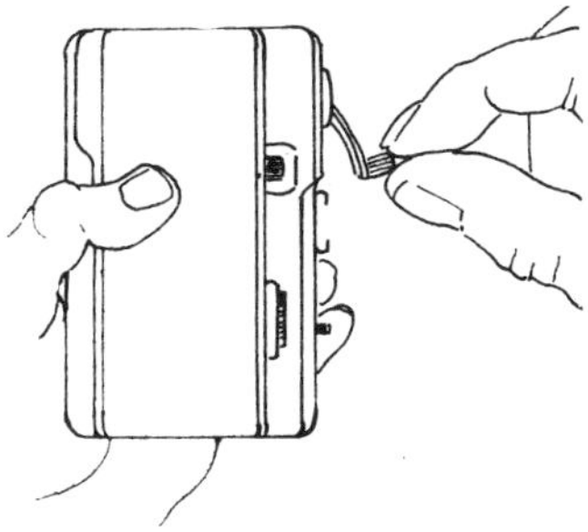

Turn rewind lever until it feels loose

When you have finished the film, wind it back into the cassette by pressing in the rewind button (normally on the bottom of the camera, but check with your instruction book) and turning the rewind lever. You will feel the film pulling slightly; when the lever feels loose and there is no more pull, you know the film is safely back in the cassette. Open the back and take it out.

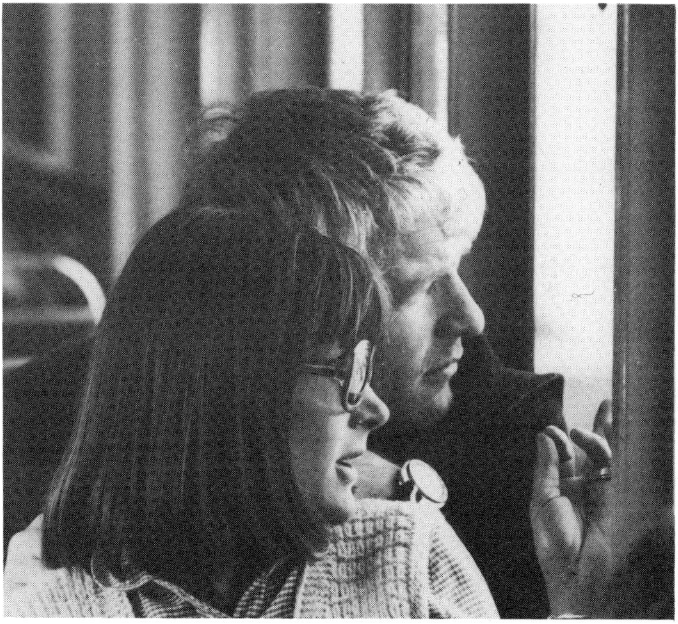

Picture taken with telephoto lens (see chapter 4).

CHAPTER 4

Lenses and Accessories

If you get carried away in the accessory department, your photography can quickly become expensive. There are a lot of photographic gadgets, and you might think that you can't take a good picture unless you have a bag bulging with bits and pieces. In fact, none of the accessories is absolutely essential. Many people take excellent pictures with cameras that won't even accept a filter, let alone a different lens. On the other hand, a few accessories can be fun to have and can also give the photographer more scope. It is best to buy slowly, deciding first what you really need.

Lenses

One advantage of owning an SLR camera is that you can take off the standard lens and fit one of a different FOCAL LENGTH. The focal length is the distance from the lens to the film when the lens is focused at infinity, and this is always described in millimetres. The focal length of a standard lens (the normal lens for a 35mm camera) is usually 50mm.

The longer the focal length, the larger the image on the film. A 150mm TELEPHOTO lens, for example, will act like a telescope and pull the thing you want to photograph closer. The final result will be an image three times larger than when the subject is photographed from the same distance with a standard lens.

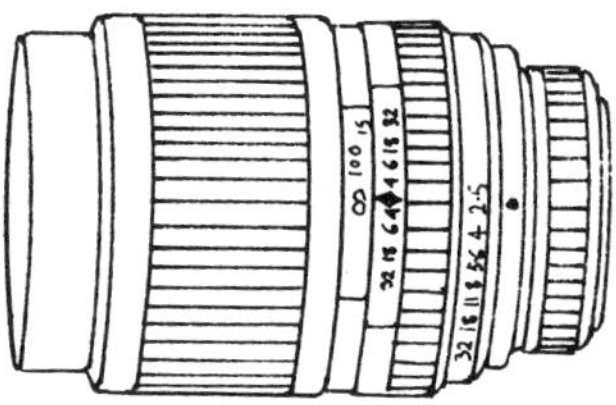

Telephoto lens

Lenses of shorter focal length than 50mm produce a smaller image, but with a wider overall view, and are known as WIDE-ANGLE lenses. This is because the focal length not only alters the size of the image, but it also changes the ANGLE OF VIEW. Look straight ahead without

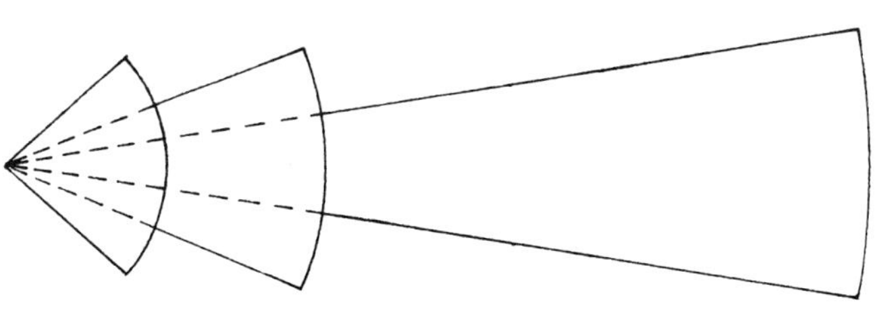

Focal lengths of standard, wide-angle and telephoto lenses

moving your eyes to left or right, and notice how much of the scene in front you can see. This is your angle of view. A standard lens has roughly the same angle of view as your eyes.

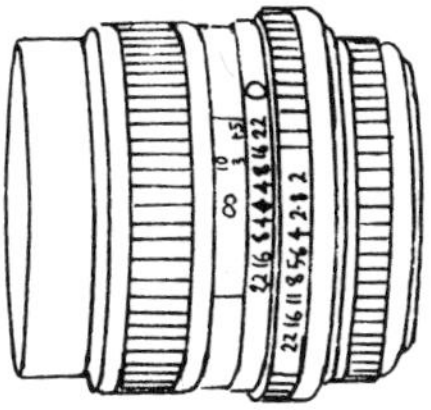

Wide-angle lens

A telephoto lens has a narrow angle of view, which means that it makes the central subject larger, but does not include the whole scene as you would see it through a standard lens (or through your own eyes). Suppose you spot a distant church surrounded by attractive countryside and think that it would make a nice picture. Your standard lens shows you a pleasant scene, but with the church looking rather insignificant. A telephoto lens will not blow the whole scene up. If you focus on the church from the same place, you will get a good-sized image of that and bring out detail, but the foreground and surrounding countryside will be cut out.

A wide-angle lens, on the other hand will include a wide expanse of countryside – far more than you saw with your standard lens – but details such as the church will look tiny and far away.

So a telephoto lens is useful for photographing objects you can't get close to, such as birds and small animals, for candid pictures of people, for sports events and other subjects if you want to isolate a particular item. A wide-angle lens is suitable for panoramic landscapes, or at times when you cannot get far enough away from a subject to include everything you want.

Telephoto lenses range from 75mm right up to enormous lenses of 1000mm. Those between 85 and 150mm are the most popular for the general photographer. The big telephotos have the disadvantage of being heavy and very long, making it difficult to hold the camera steady without resting it on something. You can also buy MIRROR lenses, which are smaller, but have long focal lengths by the use of mirrors. However, these lenses only have one aperture setting, f/3, which limits their usefulness. Telephotos have a short depth of field, and they flatten out distances, making things from the back to the front of the picture look closer together than they really are.

Wide-angle lenses have focal lengths of 20mm, 24mm, 28mm and 35mm. They have greater depth of field than standard lenses, but the very short ones can DISTORT an object (change its shape in a photograph).

If you get the chance, it is interesting to look at the same scene from the same place through different lenses. This is the best way of understanding what they all do.

If you are interested in close-up photography, such as pictures of flowers and insects, you may want to buy a MACRO lens which lets you get within centimetres of an object; some macros also magnify the object.

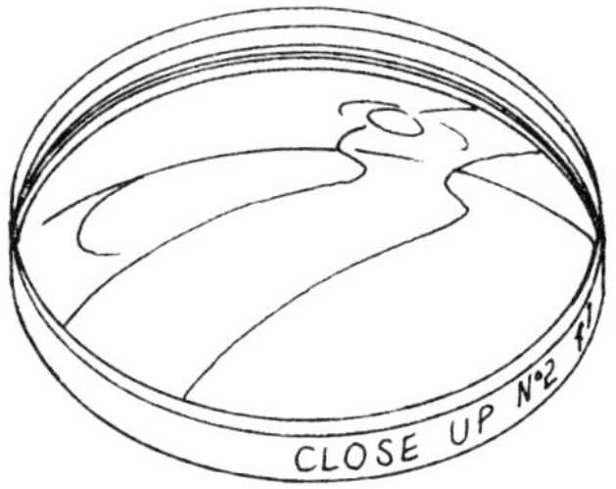

Close-up lens

Another possibility is to use a CLOSE-UP lens, which fits on to the standard lens of your camera and changes its focus, so that you can take a picture from as close as 1/4 metre.

If you have an SLR, you could also use EXTENSION TUBES or RINGS with the same sort of effect. These fit between the camera body and the lens, and change the focal length by moving the lens further away from the film.

One way of buying several focal lengths at once is to get a ZOOM lens. These are bulkier than a fixed length lens, but can be useful if you are not sure which sort of lens you need most. You can get telephoto zooms, up to about 300mm; or ones which go from wide-angle to standard and telephoto, in various combinations from

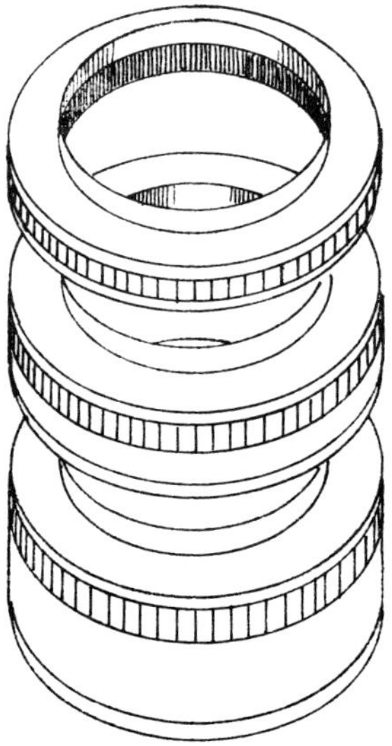

Extension tubes or rings

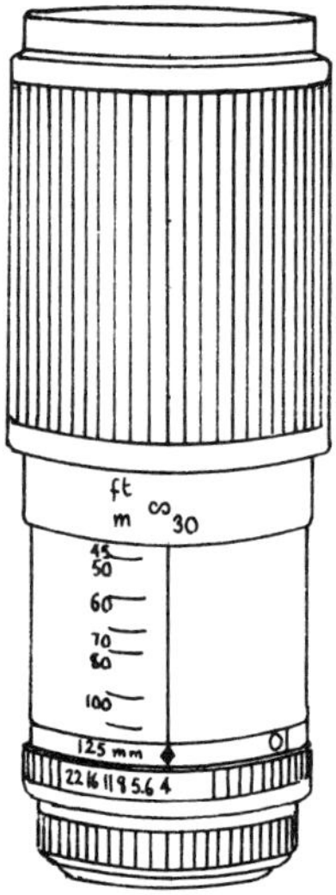

Zoom lens

28mm to 300mm. Some zoom lenses also have a macro position. You can use a zoom lens at any focal length within the range it covers; for example, between 70 and 150mm, or 28 and 100mm, and so on.

A fairly cheap method of altering focal length if you have an SLR camera is to buy a CONVERTER. A teleconverter is fitted between the lens and the camera, and magnifies the image. For example, if you use a 2X (two times) converter with a 150mm lens, you double the image size, or get the effect of a 300mm lens. A disadvantage of the converter is that it cuts down the amount of light coming into the camera, but you can allow for this by increasing the aperture size by two stops for a 2X converter, and three stops for a 3X converter. A built-in light meter will show the correct exposure. There is also a wide-angle converter, which gives a standard lens a shorter focal length.

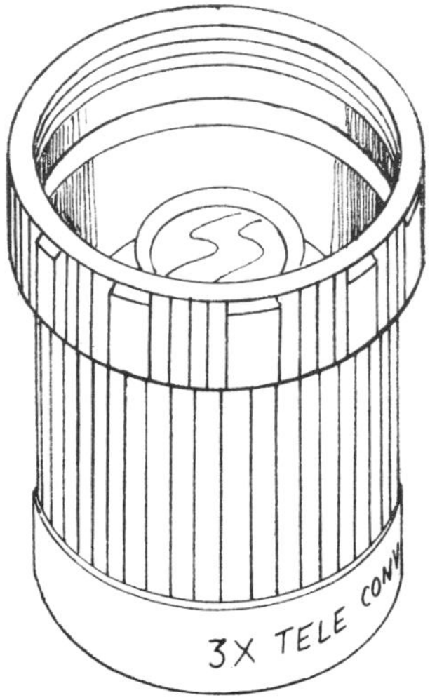

Converter for an SLR camera

A LENS HOOD shades the lens and prevents glare when you are taking pictures into the sun, and it is a good idea to use one all the time. You can buy rubber lens hoods which adapt to suit a standard, telephoto, or wide-angle lens and fold flat against the lens when the camera is stored. If you haven't got a lens hood, always keep the lens in the shade of a tree or a wall when taking pictures into the light.

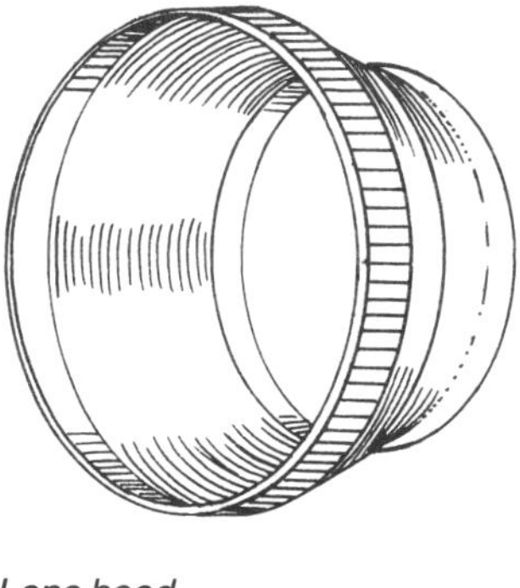

Lens hood

Filters

Filters are circles of coloured glass which fit on to the front of the lens. They are normally screwed on, though some clip on. Check at a photographic shop which type of filter your camera will take and make sure that it fits the camera before buying one.

Filters are fairly cheap accessories which can be

collected one by one as you can afford them. There is a large range available and you don't need them all. There are filters

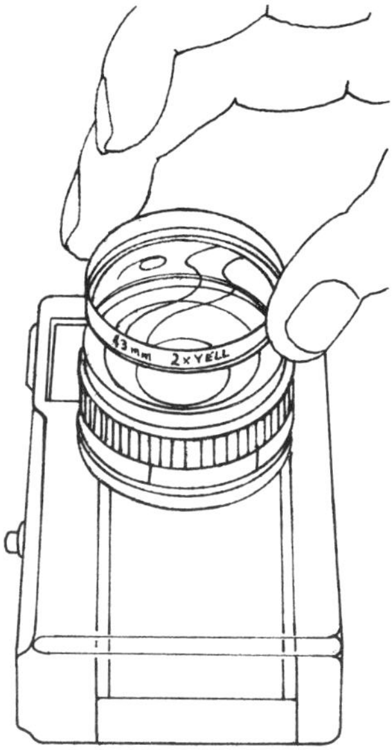

Fitting the filter on the lens cap

which increase contrast in black and white photography, or alter colour tones in colour photography, and there are special effect filters, such as a starburst, which creates the impression of stars round lights in the photograph.

Some filters may be useful even from the beginning. If you are taking pictures in black and white, you may find that they come out in tones of grey, with flat-looking skies. Yellow and orange filters bring out contrast, making clouds stand out by darkening the blue of the sky, (a red filter has an even more dramatic effect). So it may be useful to have a yellow filter on the camera for general black and white photography out of doors.

A filter will affect the amount of light entering the camera, and you have to compensate for this with increased exposure. The amount of increase is shown by the FILTER FACTOR supplied with the filter. A factor of 2 means that you need to increase exposure by one f-stop. A factor of 1 means no change to the exposure, while a factor of 8 (with a red filter, perhaps) means an increase of three f-stops. If you are using an SLR camera with built-in light meter, this should be shown in the reading, but read the instructions that come with the filter, and always remember to compensate for it, or to check that the camera is doing so. If you want to check the effect with an SLR, take a reading with and without the filter and see if there is a difference.

A UV (ultra-violet) filter is a useful one to keep on the camera all the time. It is almost clear and makes no difference to the exposure. The effect is to cut out haze, giving a crisper picture. If it is kept on the camera all the time, it will protect the lens from scratches and dirt.

Filters for colour photography do not alter the contrast. They affect the tone of some of the colours in the scene. One warms up colours on a grey day; another cools the colours of evening shots, and so on. A skylight filter is a very useful one to have, because it cuts out the overall blue tint that photographs sometimes have on a very bright day, and warms colours, without altering the exposure.

A POLARISING filter can be used for colour, and black and white photography. It works in a similar way to polarised sunglasses, cutting out glare from the sun and reflections on water, glass or polished surfaces. It also deepens the blue of the sky, so you can avoid the problem of a bright blue sky coming out almost white in a photograph because of the contrast in the scene.

There are several special effect filters to choose from, and they are mainly fun items which create effects you could not achieve otherwise. Some give an image repeated several times, others give a soft-focus effect, or frame a picture in some way, such as a VIGNETTE (see chapter 16). Have a look at the range in a camera shop to see if any appeal to you.

Tripods

A tripod is a three-legged stand to steady the camera, and is useful for night shots or other photographs that need a slow shutter speed. Tripods are collapsible and fold up into neat bags, but they are rather heavy and difficult to carry around. If you think you need a tripod, choose one that is sturdy yet fairly light, but in fact, you can often rest the camera on a table, wall or other steady surface just as easily as using a tripod. Sometimes you can brace yourself against a wall or tree, or rest the camera on a friend's shoulder to steady it.

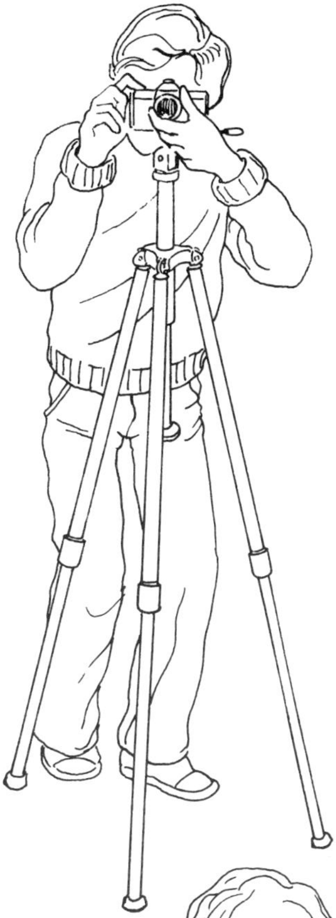

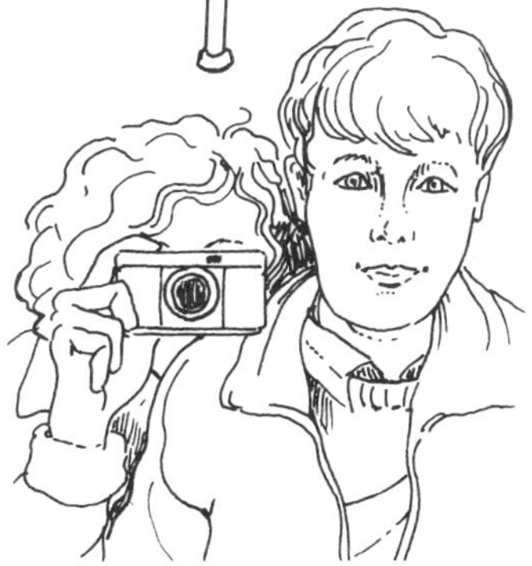

Use a tripod or friend's shoulder

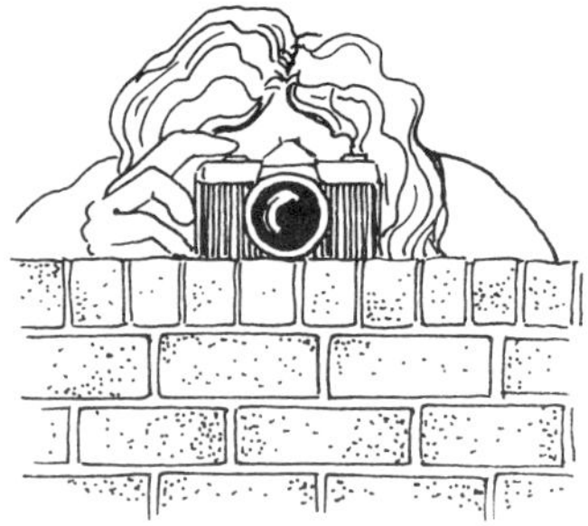

Brace yourself against a wall or tree

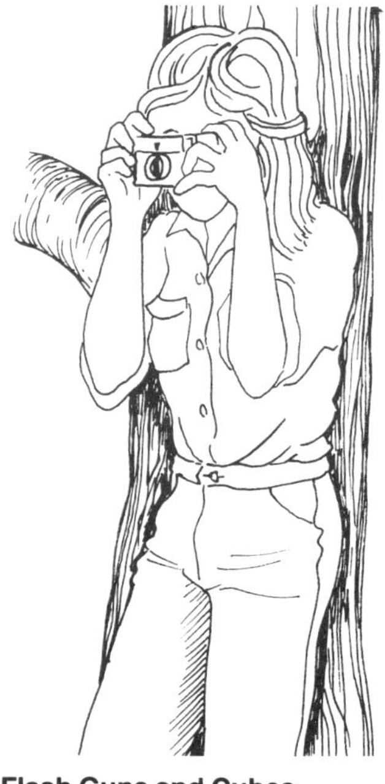

Flash Guns and Cubes

If your camera hasn't got a built-in flash gun, you may need to buy a separate one, or some flash cubes if your camera takes these. There are various types of flash guns, some straightforward point-and-flash ones, and others which allow you to bounce flash, hand-hold the flash gun off the camera and so on (see chapter 7).

Storing and Cleaning your Equipment

As you start collecting more equipment, you will need a GADGET BAG to carry it around in and protect everything from knocks and dust. Gadget bags can be simple and cheap, or they can be expensive with lots of different pockets and pouches for lenses and accessories. Don't buy one until you have a good idea of how much equipment you plan to get. It is irritating to buy a new bag and then find you can't squeeze everything in. Protect your camera in its own case in the meantime, and always keep a lens cap on the lens when you are not taking a picture.

If you do buy a gadget bag, make sure it is lightweight, but with plenty of protective padding. Don't buy a very large bag if you plan to do a lot of walking around with your camera. Carrying it will make your shoulder ache and may put you off taking your photographic gear around with you.

You will need cleaning equipment for your camera and lenses, and this can also be kept in your bag. A blower brush for cleaning dust off the lens is important. You can buy cleaning kits which include a blower brush, duster and cleaning liquids for lens and body, or you can simply use a brush and soft cloth for this. Never use anything but a soft, fluff-free cloth and a proper lens brush to clean a lens as it is easily scratched.

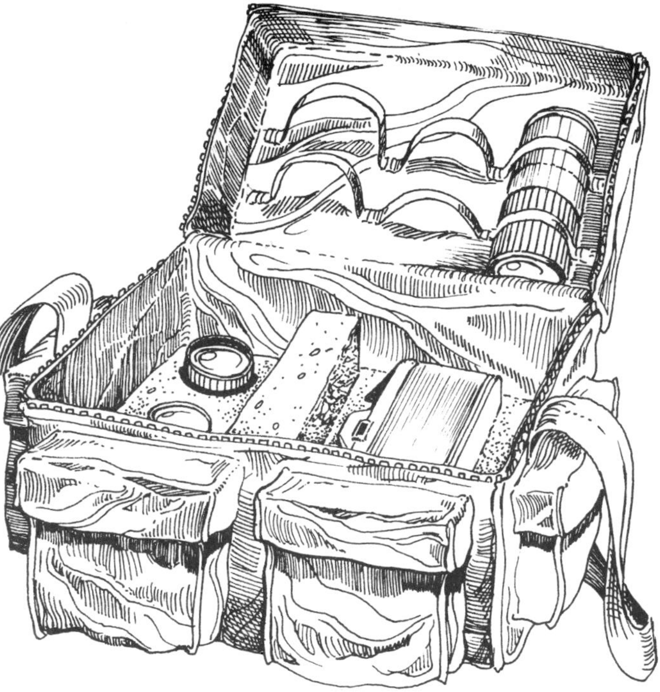

A gadget bag protects your camera and equipment

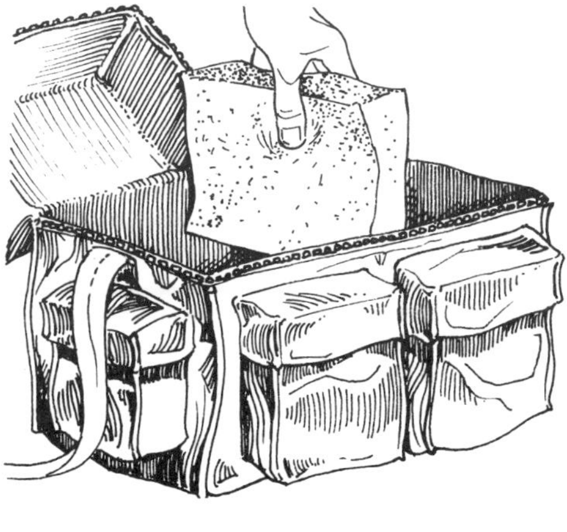

Use foam to make compartments in the bag

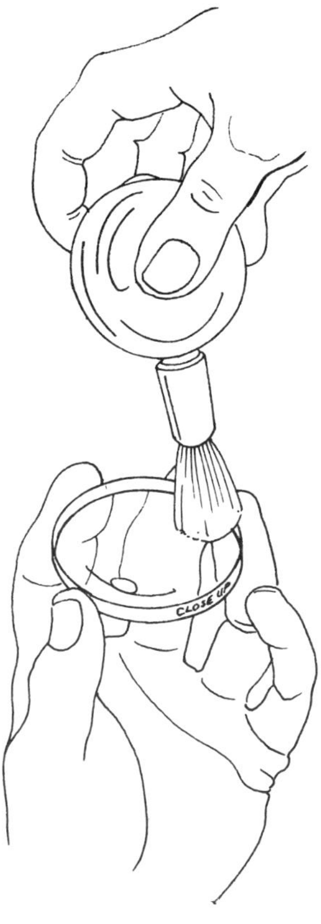

A blower brush for cleaning lenses

It is important to look after your equipment carefully, and keeping it clean is part of this. Dust on the lens will show on photographs, for one thing; for another, no machine works well if it is clogged up with dust and dirt, and it could be permanently damaged. Always protect your camera and equipment from dust and dirt by keeping them zipped up in a bag, on a shelf or in a cupboard rather than on the floor, when you are not using them.

You may prefer to buy a large bag for your camera and then divide it into compartments yourself when you get more equipment. You can use foam rubber as padding. Design the layout you want and make careful measurements. Cut the foam into pieces to make divisions, or complete wrap-around protection for lenses. You can stitch the foam pieces together, or attach Velcro to them so that you can change the positioning as you get more gadgets. Another idea is to use a thick piece of foam rubber as a base for your bag, and scoop out areas with a sharp knife to take your lenses and other equipment. The main thing is to stop them knocking together in the bag, which will damage them.

If your bag has a lid, you can attach loops of elastic to it for small bits and pieces, such as your notebook and pencil. Arrange your bag so that it is easy to find your gadgets and get them out without having to rearrange everything.

CHAPTER 5

Using your Camera

When you have looked at all the different controls on your camera,

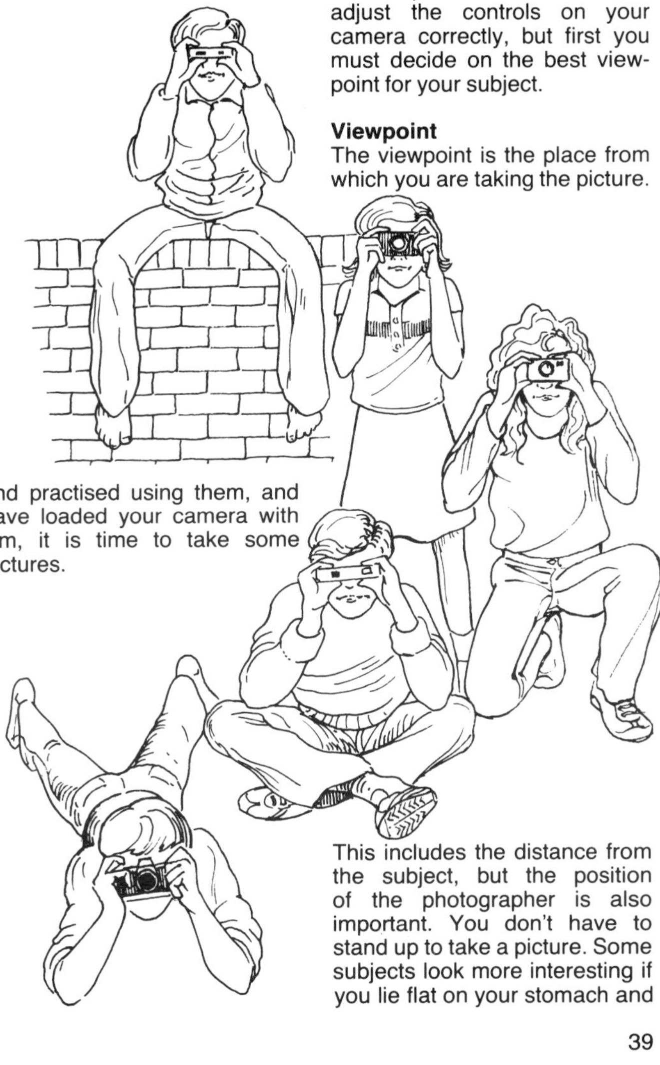

and practised using them, and have loaded your camera with film, it is time to take some pictures.

You will need a SUBJECT (something you would like to photograph). It is easier to practise with stationary (still) subjects, because there is time to think about what you are doing without panic. You will need to adjust the controls on your camera correctly, but first you must decide on the best viewpoint for your subject.

Viewpoint

The viewpoint is the place from which you are taking the picture. This includes the distance from the subject, but the position of the photographer is also important. You don't have to stand up to take a picture. Some subjects look more interesting if you lie flat on your stomach and look up at them. A low-level viewpoint is best for a picture of a field of flowers, a small animal, or a child playing on the ground. (If you stand up and look down on the subject, you are further away from it, and it may be distorted.)

Some subjects look more impressive if you photograph them from above. In a town, for example, you can sometimes get a striking view of a building or a street by climbing up to the top of a high building.

So think about your subject and the best viewpoint for it. You could stand, sit, squat down, kneel, lie on the ground, or climb up high. If you get into the habit of trying to look for an interesting viewpoint for pictures, you can often make good use of a subject that does not look worthy of a photograph at first glance.

Horizontal or Vertical?

Another point to think about is whether to take a horizontal (sideways) or a vertical (upright) picture. People often take horizontal pictures because it is

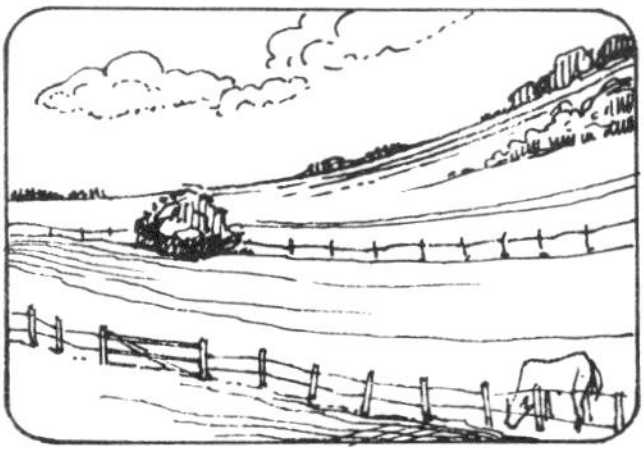

A horizontal picture

more comfortable to hold a camera that way. It can be more difficult to turn a camera on its side and find the controls, but many pictures do look better in a vertical frame, so practise this until you feel comfortable.

Usually, a tall subject looks better in a vertical frame. You can judge this for yourself. Ask a friend to stand some distance away from you. Look through the viewfinder with the camera held normally. Even if you are careful not to waste any space at top and bottom, and get close enough for your friend to fill the picture that way, there will be wasted space at the sides. You can only get as close as the height of the frame permits, so your friend looks small and isolated with a lot of unimportant landscape on either side.

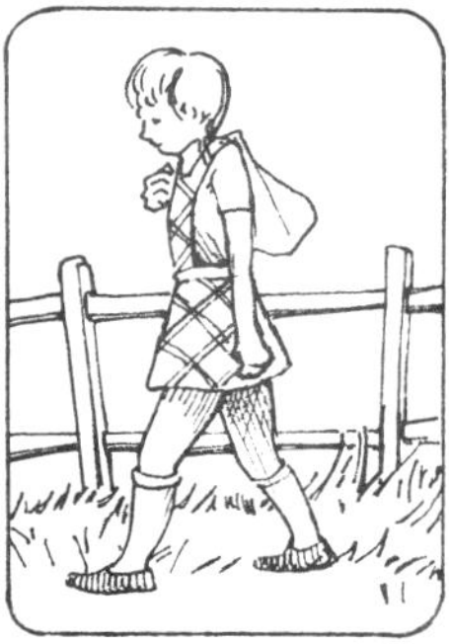

A vertical picture

Now turn the camera to the vertical position. Frame the picture so that your friend's head is near the top of the viewfinder and his feet are near the bottom. This time you will see a bigger image of your friend, with very little wasted space anywhere.

Taking a Picture

First check that you have loaded the camera with film, set the film speed dial and wound the film on ready for the next shot.

Now to set up your camera. Take a light reading for your subject and decide on the exposure combination you want to use. Set this on the camera. Frame the picture in the viewfinder from your chosen viewpoint and focus carefully on the subject until it is sharp. Check that the depth of field is what you want. (If you can't focus your camera, judge the distance and make sure you have enough depth of field to cover it. With a 110 or 126 camera, check that you are not too close to the subject.) Look at the subject through the viewfinder again and check that you are completely happy with your picture.

Look round the frame in the viewfinder and make sure that nothing is so close to the edge that it may be chopped off in the print. Check that there is no litter lying around, and that there aren't any oddities like chimneys or trees growing out of people's

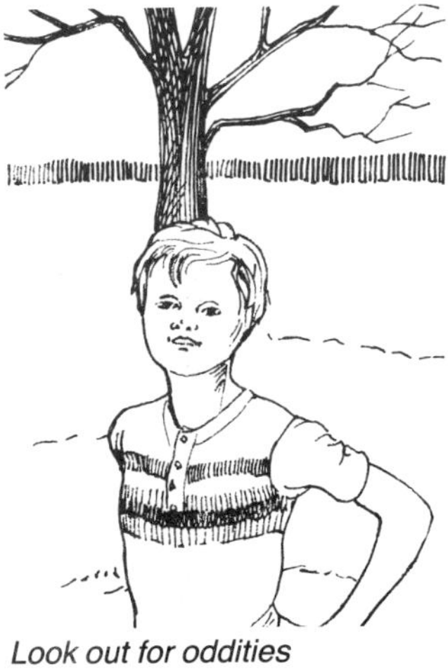

Look out for oddities

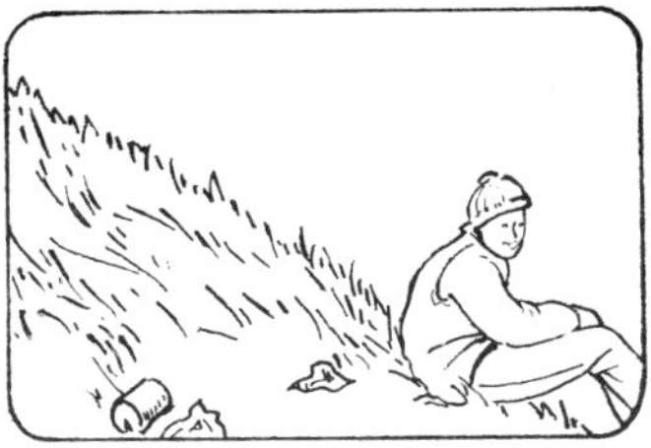

Check all round the frame

heads. Look very carefully, because it is easy to miss small things which can ruin a picture.

Think about the position of the sun (see chapter 7). Make sure that it is not shining into the lens, and that your own shadow is not included in the picture.

If your camera has a direct viewfinder, you may not notice things in front of the lens, such as your fingers or the strap of your camera case, and these will come out as black shapes in the picture. So make sure that there is nothing in front of the lens to spoil the picture.

When you are ready to take the picture, hold the camera

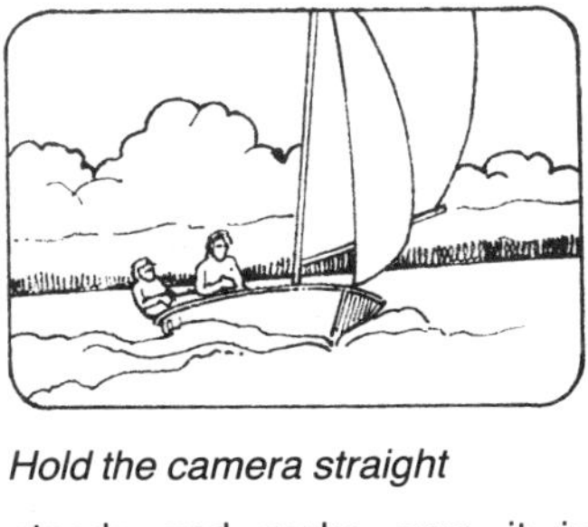

Hold the camera straight

steady and make sure it is straight. If it is held at a slant, you will get a sloping horizon, which looks very peculiar. Keep your elbows tucked in to help steady your arms. It is possible to get camera shake and a blurred picture even with speeds over 1/30, so do take care. If you are worried, steady yourself or your camera against a wall, a chair back or some other firm surface. Make sure that you feel comfortable with the way you are holding your camera before you take the picture.

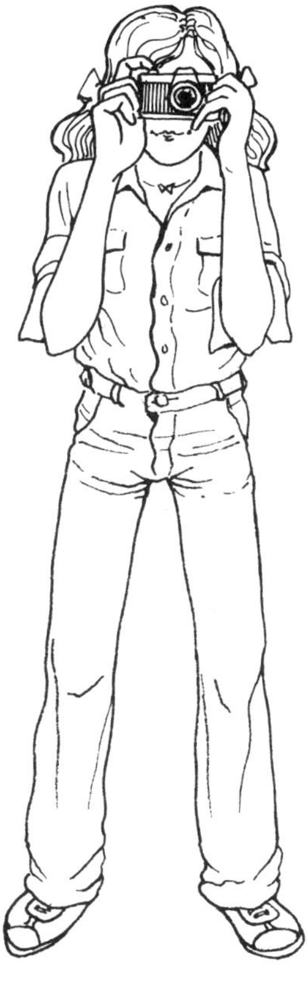

Make sure you feel comfortable before taking a picture

Press the shutter release smoothly and slowly, taking care not to jerk the camera as you do so. When you have taken the picture, wind the film on ready for the next shot.

If you have a 110 or a fully automatic camera, you won't need to do things like setting exposures, of course, but you still have to concentrate on framing the picture, holding the camera and taking the picture smoothly. Again, practice makes perfect. If you feel awkward holding your camera, the chances are that you will shake it at the crucial moment and get a blurred picture. As you gain experience, the routine for setting up your camera and taking a picture will become second nature to you. To start with, take your time and practise each step carefully. Correct exposure and sharp focusing are important, but so are all the other stages.

If you have an adjustable camera, it is useful to keep it set on a general exposure combination ready for those moments when you see a picture and haven't the time to take a light reading. You need a fairly small aperture, such as f/11, to give you depth of field, and one of the faster shutter speeds, such as 1/125 or 1/250, to avoid problems with camera shake and movement if you are working quickly. When you go out for a day's photography, take a general light reading for the film speed you are using and choose a pair of aperture and shutter speed settings which are suitable for the film and the conditions. It is, of course, better to take individual readings when you can, but it is frustrating to miss that once-in-a-lifetime picture because the subject moved away while you were setting up your camera.

These are the basic rules for taking a picture. You need to follow rules even with a simple camera with no adjustable controls, otherwise photography is worrying rather than enjoyable. Will that picture come out? Should I have given it more exposure? Did I shake the camera? Did I check the frame properly, or was that bit of drainpipe or that tin lying there all the time? If you work out a procedure for your camera and run through it every time you take a picture, you will know that you did everything. Getting the best exposure and using the controls does take practise, but anyone can see a tin or a paper bag lying on the ground!

It is a good idea to have a notebook and pencil with you to make a note of the exposure combinations you used for each picture. Then, if the print doesn't look quite right, you can work out where you are going wrong, and if it looks perfect, you can remember what you did for next time!

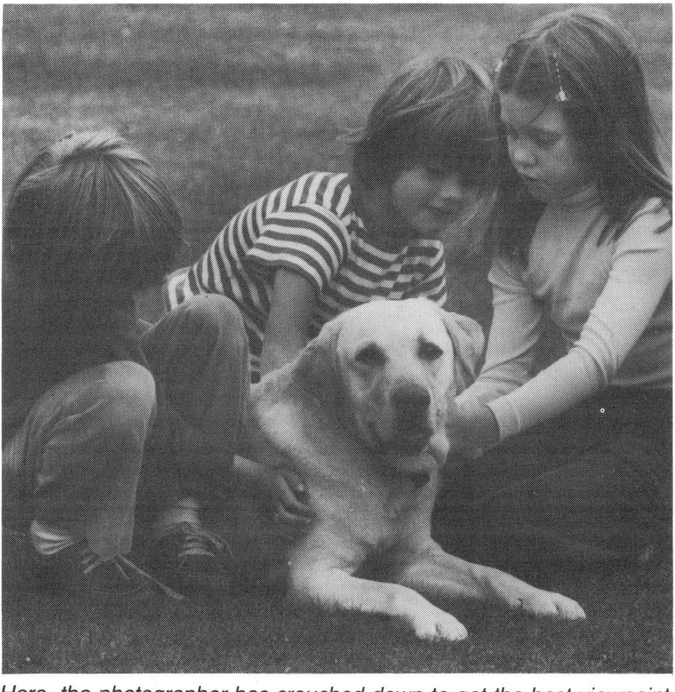

Here, the photographer has crouched down to get the best viewpoint of the group

CHAPTER 6

Composing a Picture

When you take a photograph, it may be disappointing unless you pay a lot of attention to the COMPOSITION (the positions of things in the picture). This may seem obvious, but pictures don't always come out as you expect them to. A scene which looks attractive to the human eye can look flat and boring in a photograph. On the other hand, a subject which looks boring in real life can make a striking picture.

The Background

The background is very important. If it is too fussy, it will distract the eye from the main subject, but a well-chosen background can make a subject even more interesting.

How much background should you have? This depends on the subject. As a general rule, it is best to fill the frame as much as possible with your subject, so the background is just there to fill in the bits round the edge. Sometimes, though, the background is part of the subject. For example, if you are on holiday, you may want to take a picture of your family or friends against a background of the holiday resort. In this case, you would include more background to give an idea of what the place was like.

It is important to decide what your picture is really of, or the viewer will be muddled. Is it of the person or is it of the place? If it is of the place, with the person positioned to lead the eye into the photograph or fill up an

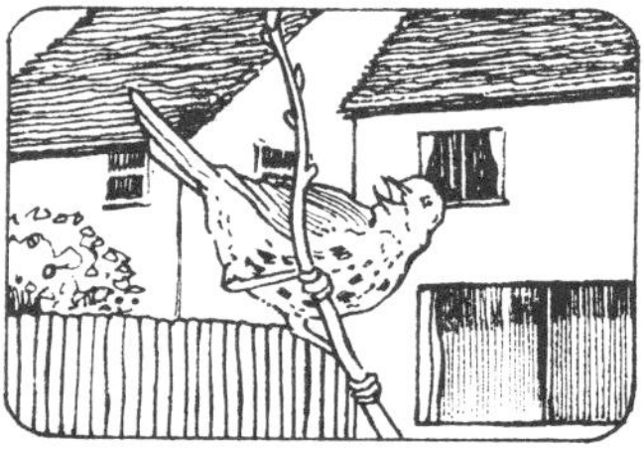

Cluttered background

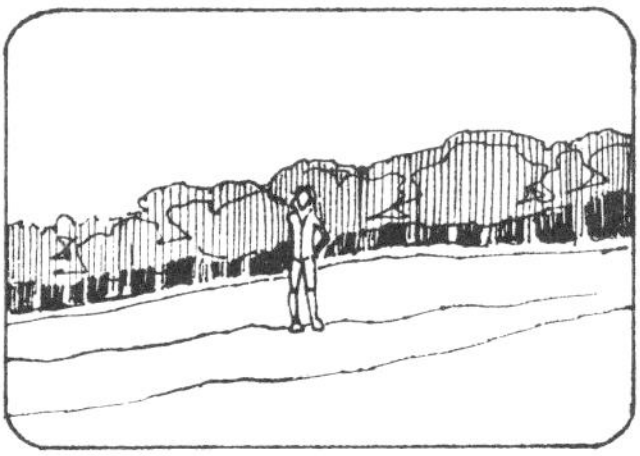

Subject too far away

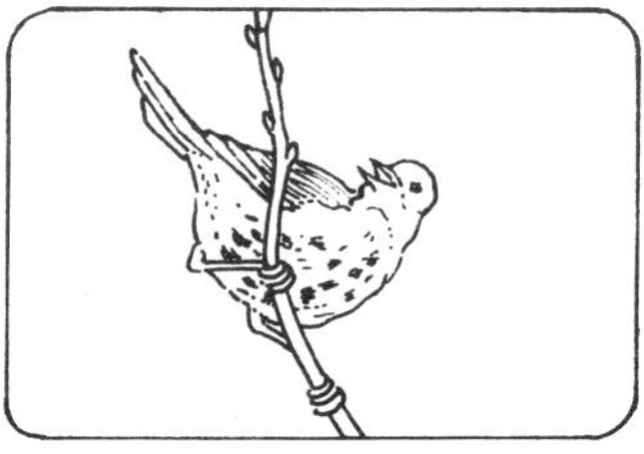

Clear background

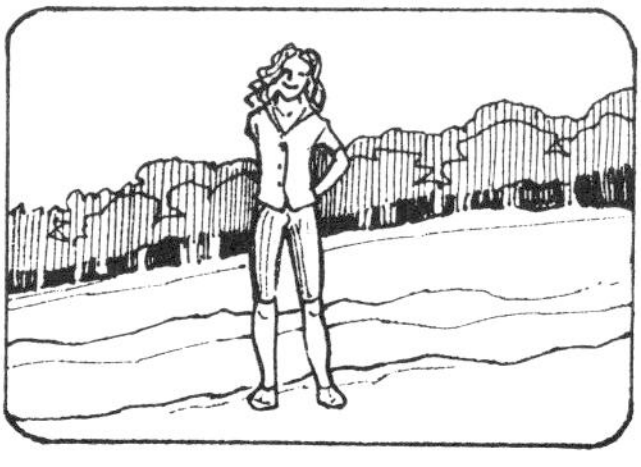

Subject better positioned

empty foreground, the place should take up most of the picture. If the person is the subject, you must be close enough to make him the main item of interest. A picture of Mum and the Eiffel Tower will confuse if you try and make them both of equal importance.

If you are taking a picture of people or animals, it is usually best to choose a plain background, such as grass, sky or a plain wall, so that the subject stands out.

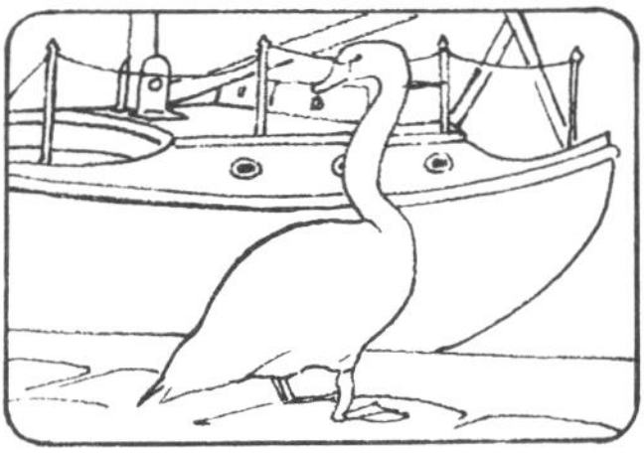

Find a better viewpoint

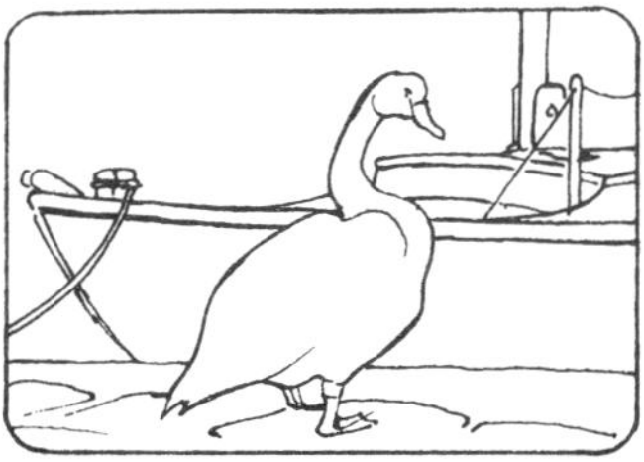

You can't always choose your background, but you can alter your viewpoint. If you find that the background is distracting, try changing it by crouching down, moving round to get a different angle, or taking a picture from above. Don't be satisfied with a cluttered background just because it is there. It will look even worse in a photograph.

Another thing to check is that there is nothing unwanted in the background, particularly if you are taking a picture with long depth of field, and make sure that everything in the picture is in character. A charming view of a country cottage will be spoilt by television aerials, wires, drainpipes, someone pegging out the

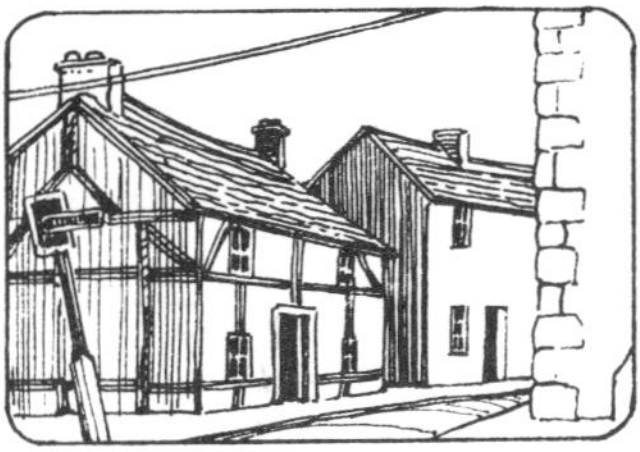

Move around if necessary

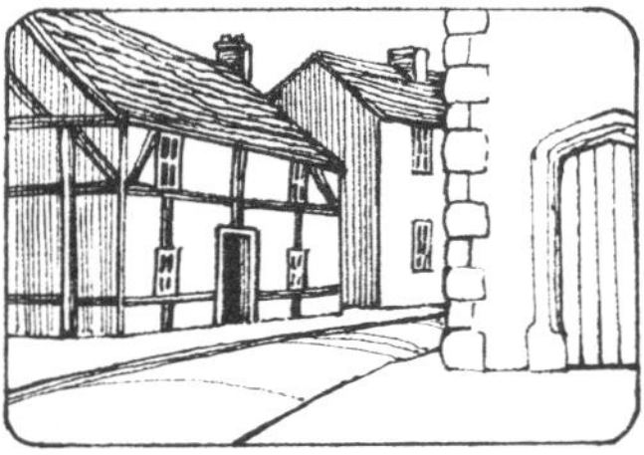

washing or cleaning the windows, a car parked outside, or other modern-day things of this kind. Try moving round to cut them out of the picture.

You can, of course, put the background out of focus. This is useful for portraits, close-ups of flowers and other subjects where you can't find a suitable background or where any recognisable background would be distracting and spoil the picture. It is a good way of isolating a subject (making it stand out on its own).

You need to use a large aperture to cut down the depth of field, so you must get close to the subject and focus carefully on it. Check your depth of field scale to make sure that the aperture is not too large to have the whole subject in focus. Take a careful light reading. You will probably need a fast shutter speed to prevent over-exposure with a very large aperture, but this depends on the subject, and how dark or light it is.

Pictures with an out-of-focus background are effective, and it is worth practising to see what subjects look best when treated like this.

The Foreground

The foreground is the area in front of the subject, and it is unfortunately a part of the picture that is often forgotten. It is easy to focus on your subject, check the background, and completely forget that there is an empty stretch of road or grass in front. You are looking at the subject and your eyes tend to skip over the foreground, but this won't happen in the picture. The foreground will be only too obvious.

If you must have quite a lot of foreground – in a landscape, for instance – make sure that there is something in it to add interest and lead the eye into the picture. For example, if your subject is a valley with a village in the middle distance and hills in the background, everything will look flat and distant if there is a large empty foreground. Try to include a tree, building or piece of farm machinery in the foreground, at one side of the picture. This adds

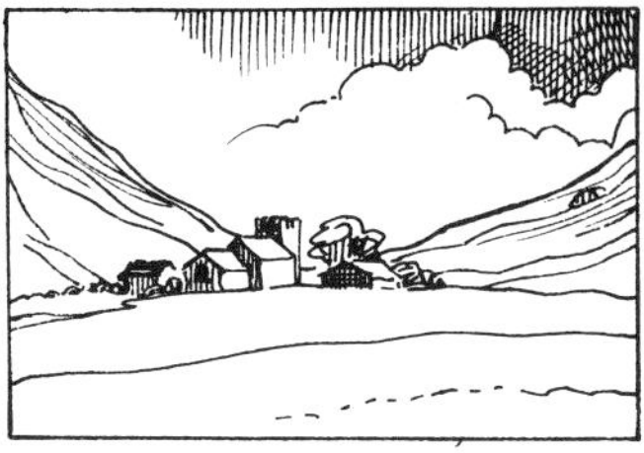

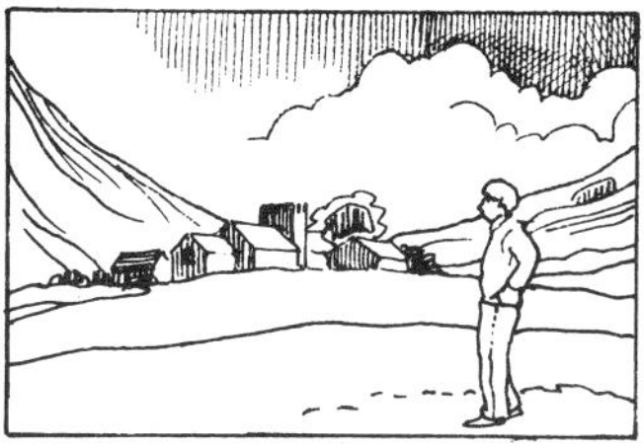

The addition of the person has added perspective

interest and also gives the picture PERSPECTIVE (a sense of distance). Photography tends to flatten out perspective, which is one of the reasons that scenes which look interesting to the human eye don't always live up to expectations in photographs. If there is nothing handy to include in the foreground, you could ask a friend to stand to one side of the picture, but make sure that he is looking into the picture – down at the village, for example. If he is looking in the other direction, this will lead the eye away from the subject.

Another way of leading the eye into the picture is to include a road, a fence, a railway line, or a hedge running from the foreground to the subject in the middle distance.

Framing a scene is an effective way of dealing with foreground and perspective problems, too. It can also fill up an uninteresting sky. In the countryside, overhanging branches, or sprays of leaves at the edges of a picture will set off a distant scene. Archways, doors and gateways do the same for buildings and street scenes. Grasses or shrubs at ground level can be used for

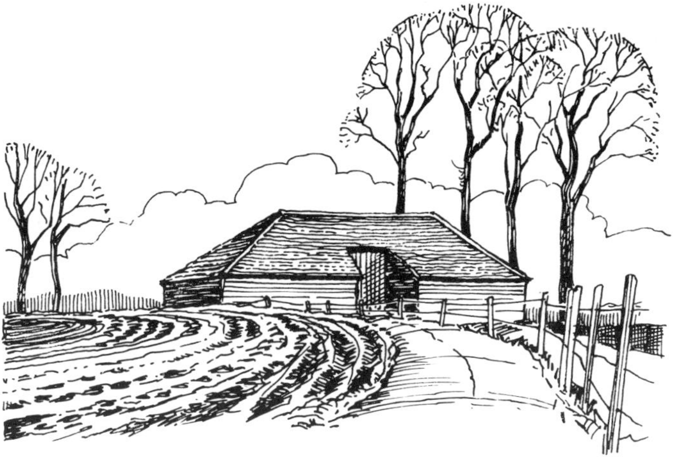

The road leads the eye into the picture

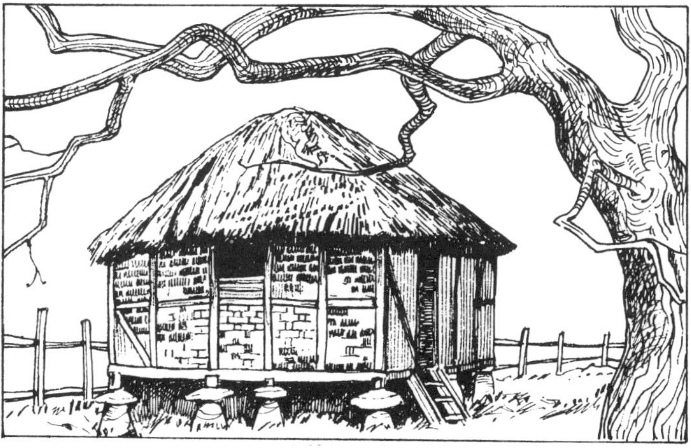

The branches effectively frame the subject

framing some subjects if you crouch down low so that you are at their level.

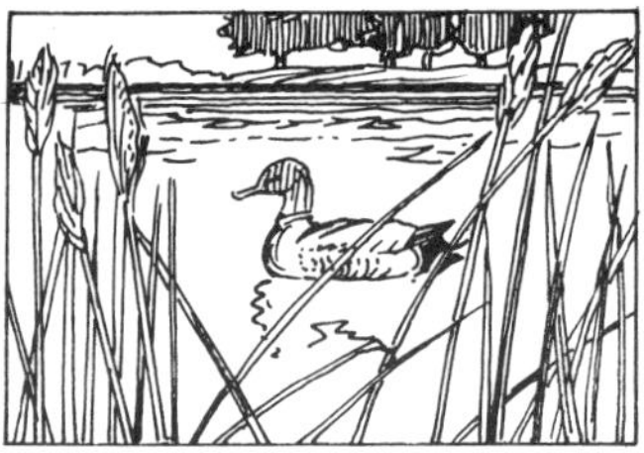

The reeds frame the duck

The frame is close to the camera and the subject is distant, so you have to decide what to focus on. It is often best to have both the distant scene and the frame in focus, but you can experiment with an out-of-focus frame of spring leaves, for example, or a sharp framework of branches with a slightly hazy view. Once again, it depends what you want your picture to show. Be careful, though, because things like that can look like mistakes.

The main thing about the foreground is to remember that it is there. When you are composing a picture in the viewfinder, look from the bottom of the frame right up to the subject and judge how much foreground there is, whether it is too much and, if this is unavoidable, whether there is something of interest in it.

Finding a Focal Point

You may have taken pictures that have come out looking a jumbled mess, and wondered where you went wrong. If you point your camera at a busy street scene, a distant view, or a crowd of people and take a picture, the effect will be a jumble. The eye doesn't know what to look at and isn't particularly interested in anything it sees.

Every picture needs a FOCAL POINT – a main item of interest

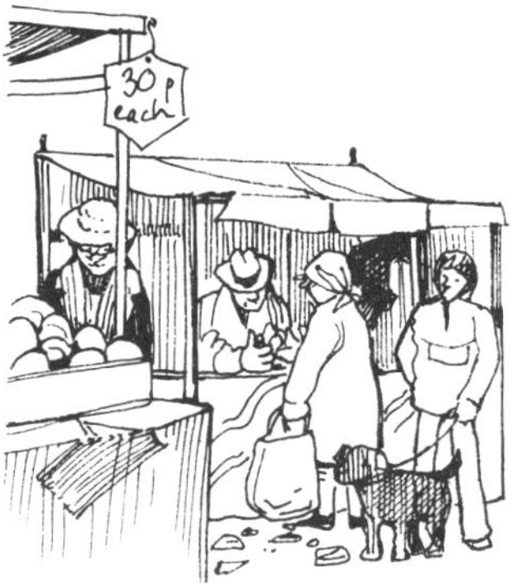

The picture is too cluttered

that sets off the surrounding scene. Suppose you want a picture of a busy market. The scene looks bright and interesting to you. When this picture is printed, it is a mess. There are people walking in all directions,

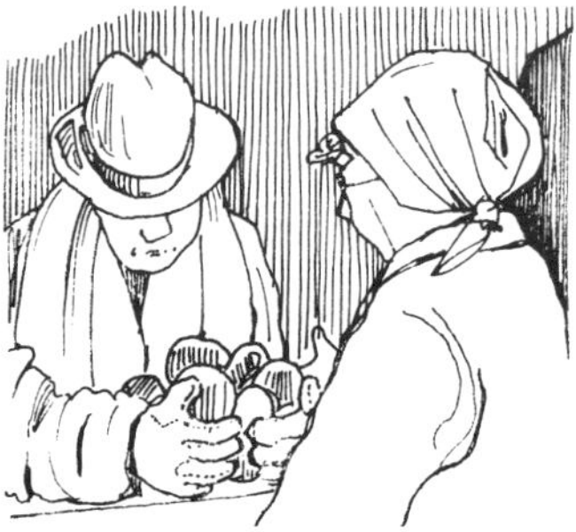

Pick out a focal point

none of the stalls is really clear, people have been masked by other people walking in front of them, and so on. You are more likely to get a successful picture if you choose one stall as your focal point. Wait until the people selling and buying at this particular stall are in a good position for a picture, focus carefully on the fruit and vegetables or whatever, and the result is an interesting market scene with plenty of life and colour, and no confusion.

The focal point can be in the foreground, or the middle distance. In a landscape, for example, you may lead the eye nicely into the picture with a road or a river, but if there is no focal point the effect will be disappointing. The eye should be led to a church, bridge, or house, an interesting hill, or something that stands out from the rest of the scene. A bleak hillside landscape can be made into a picture by a single tree on the horizon, a lone sheep grazing, a fence along the skyline, or even a rock in the foreground. It doesn't really matter what or where it is, so long as you remember that it is not enough to see a pretty view and hope it will make a good picture. Always think, 'Background, foreground, focal point', and make sure they are all taken care of before you press the shutter release.

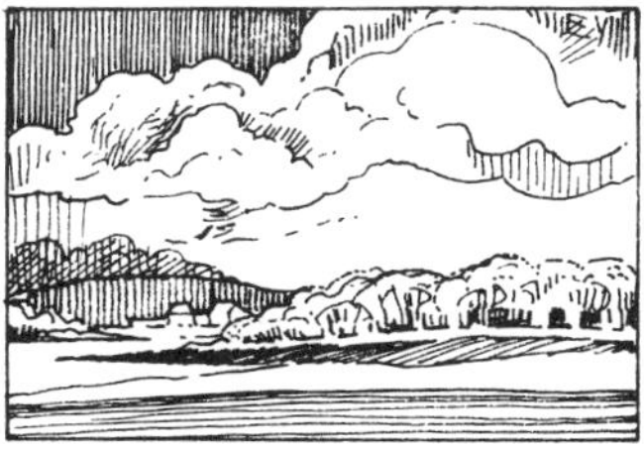

Keep the horizon low for a dramatic effect

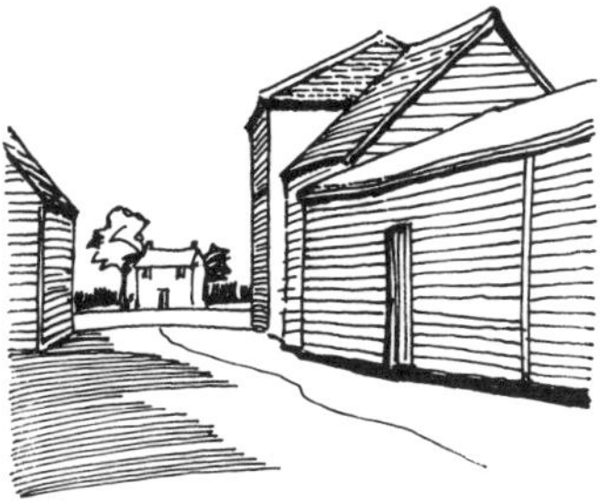

Lead the eye into the picture

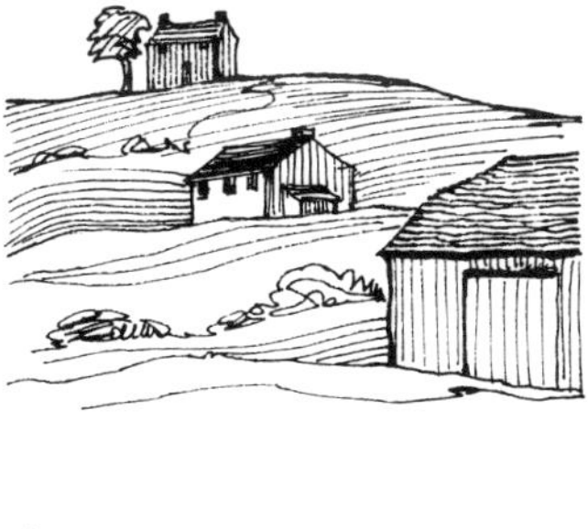

Don't let anything cut the picture in half – either the focal point or the horizon. The focal point should be positioned on one side or the other, however slightly, rather than in the middle of the frame, and the horizon should be above or below the halfway mark, depending on the subject and how important you want the sky to be. For example, an interesting sky can be made more dramatic by having the horizon fairly low.

Framing the Subject

The composition of your picture depends on the subject, as we have seen, but remember to fill the frame. If you are taking a picture with a person as the main subject, get in close so that that person really takes up the space. Don't be content to have a dot in the distance and call it a picture of Uncle Joe. The same applies

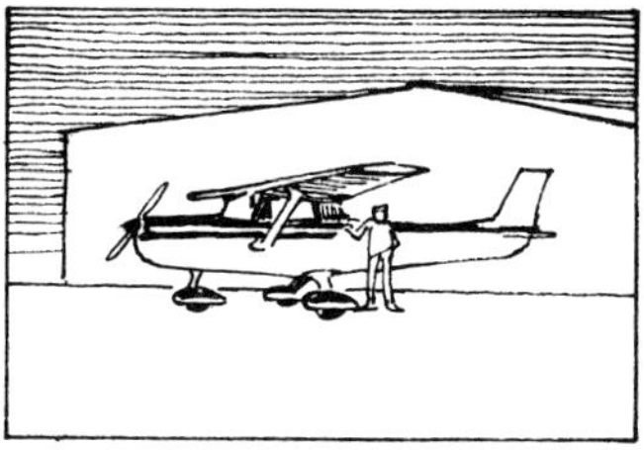

The photographer is too far away

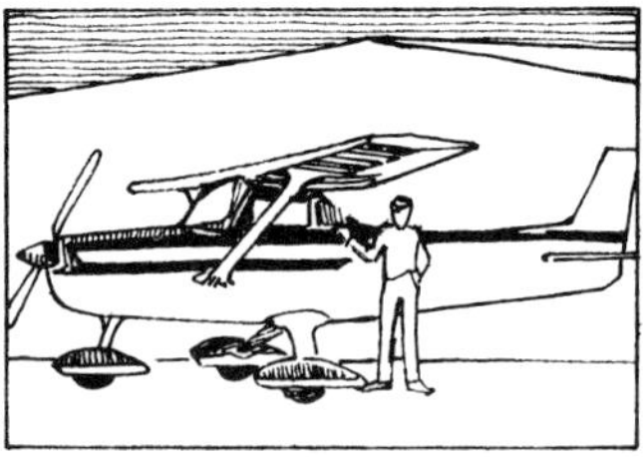

Moving closer to the subject gives a better picture

with animals, or any other single item. Get as close as you possibly can, keeping the subject within the frame, so that there are the minimum of gaps around the edges. Things tend to look smaller on the finished print, so that even if something seems a reasonable size in the viewfinder, the chances are that it will be lost in the final picture if you are too far away.

Practise framing subjects in the viewfinder without taking pictures. You may be surprised at how close you have to go to fill the frame. Get rid of unwanted foreground and make sure there isn't wasted space at the sides, if you can. Obviously, the shape of your subject will also affect this – a tall thin subject may fill the frame top and bottom, but leave space at the sides, even with a vertical shot – and you won't always want to be this close for every subject. But if you get into the habit of thinking, 'Fill the frame', you won't make the mistake of thinking something is large enough when it only takes up half the space available.

If you are taking a picture of someone walking through a wood, say, and want to show part of the wood to give atmosphere, it will still look better if the person is not too small. Experiment with a vertical frame to see if the height of the trees adds to the composition. Make sure that the person is recognisable, if he is your main subject, and that he isn't lost among leaves and branches, and doesn't look as though he is there by mistake. There will still be room for plenty of surrounding woodland.

When you have composed your picture, remember to make sure that there is nothing that would spoil the photograph, and change your position if you need to. Check the ground and the foreground right down to the edge of the frame. Make sure that nothing is so near the edge of the frame that it could be cut off in the final print, particularly if you have a direct viewfinder.

All this sounds hard work, but takes only a few seconds once you have got a checklist in your mind.

CHAPTER 7

Lighting

Lighting is probably the most important thing to consider in photography. Without good lighting, a photograph will not be a success, however interesting the subject, but dramatic or unusual lighting can make even a very ordinary subject look different and new.

The Sun

When you are taking photographs out of doors, you will normally be relying on light from the sun. Sunlight not only provides enough light to give you a choice of exposure settings, but it also gives the scene the highlights and shadows it needs. It brings out colours in colour photography, and crisp black and white tones in black and white photography. Pictures taken on a cloudy day will often look flat and dull because there are no shadows and the colours have no brilliance.

So it is worth thinking carefully about light from the beginning. Even before you take a picture, study a subject – a building, for example – at different times of the day. Notice the difference in the colours from morning to evening light, and the difference the angle of the sun makes to shadows, shapes and TEXTURES (surfaces).

In the early morning, as the sun comes up, the light has more pink in it than later in the day. Bright sunlight adds a blue tone to the light, while late afternoon and evening sunlight have a warm reddish glow. These changes in colour can be used to help to express the mood.

Look at the same scene on a sunny day and then on a cloudy day. Notice how everything looks flat when the weather is cloudy. You can take pictures on cloudy days, of course, but you need bold shapes or contrasts in

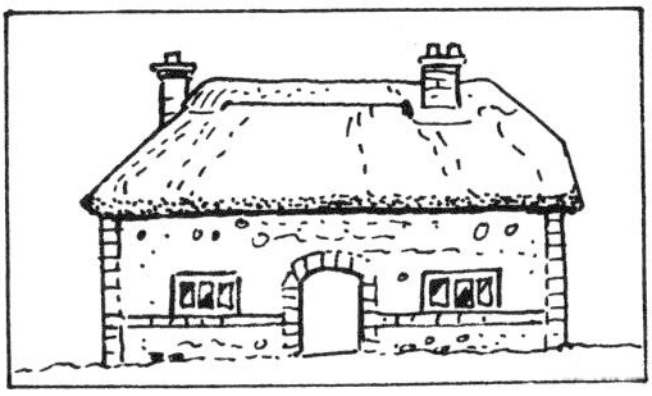

1 Front lighting

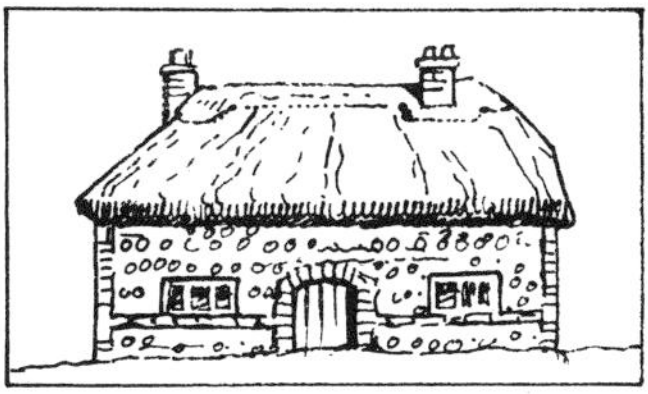

2 Half-side lighting

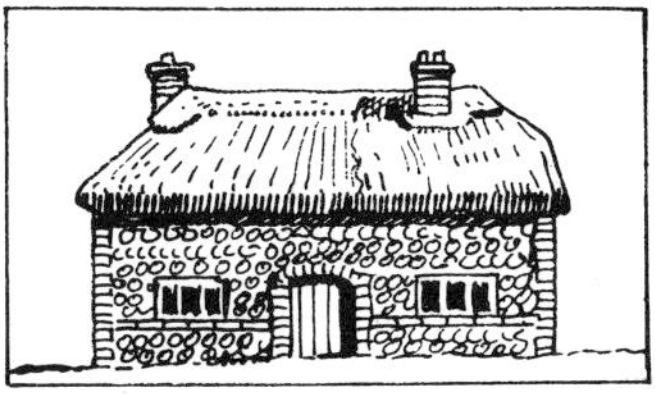

3 Side lighting

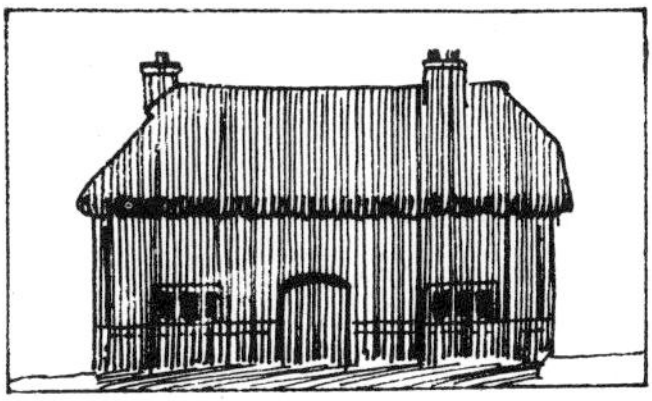

4 Back lighting

colour, or some other interesting feature to make up for the lack of shadow and highlight. Sometimes light reflected from water – a river or even a rain puddle – can provide highlights on a cloudy day. At times, of course, you may *want* a sombre picture with soft colours, but it is important to learn to recognise the different conditions so that you get what you really want and are not disappointed with the final picture.

The direction of the light is also important, particularly in black and white photography, where you are relying on shadows, shape and texture to give your subject life. There is nothing mysterious about this. You can see it with your own eyes. Look at a building at different times of day, as the sun swings round, and try to pick out the changes.

Front Lighting

When the sun is behind you, it casts a bright, flat light on the subject. This brings out colour, but not shape and texture. The shadows are light. Front lighting, as this is called, is good for colour pictures in which the most important thing is to show bright colours, like reds and yellows. It is less good for black and white photographs, as lack of shadow and detail will make the subject look flat.

If you use front lighting for pictures of people looking at the camera, they will tend to squint because the sun is shining in their eyes.

Half-Side (45°) Lighting

This is known as 'sun over the left shoulder' lighting. The sun is not immediately behind you, but slightly to one side. The shadows will be deeper and the shapes of buildings and the texture of the stone will show up more. This lighting is good for black and white photography, as the shadows are dark and the contrast sharpens up the picture. The subject begins to look three-dimensional rather than flat.

With colour, though, the increase in contrast can cause problems, because colour film cannot cope well with a broad range of light and shade. Very deep shadows will come out black on a colour picture, which can spoil the overall effect. So use this lighting with care. If there are dark shadows and bright surfaces, you may have to make a series of exposure readings and decide which would be the best combination for bringing out detail without too much harsh shadow.

Side Lighting

When the sun is shining on a subject from one side, texture is brought out most strongly of all, so side lighting is good for black and white and colour photography of subjects where texture is important. Beware of shadows created by side lighting. These will be thrown straight across the picture, and you may get shadows from things outside the frame, such as trees and other buildings. Always think of this when composing your picture. Notice where the shadows fall, and also which parts of your subject are in shadow and which in light. The use of side lighting is very effective, and can even be dramatic, if the subject is right.

Back Lighting

If the sun is behind the subject, you will see a SILHOUETTE (see illustration). This is called back lighting, and the effect will

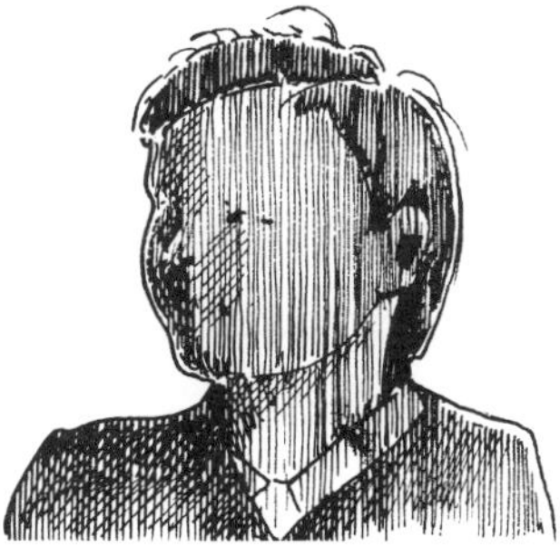

be even stronger on a photograph. You can use back lighting for colour, and black and white, and the silhouette technique can be used with various subjects, but make sure you only get it when you want it! Don't take a picture into the sun if you want to see a subject's face, for example.

Choice of lighting of course depends on the subject. For a colourful scene in which you want to bring out bold colours, front lighting is best. For subjects where the texture and shape are important, use half-side or side lighting. This is especially important for black and white photography, and when the subject has a curved or roughly textured surface. If you want the subject to be in silhouette – boats against water, perhaps, or people walking along a beach or skyline – use back lighting.

Colour

While thinking about composition and light, it is important to consider colour too. If you are choosing an outfit of clothes, you think about the colours of each item, whether they clash and whether different shades tone in with each other. It is the same with colours in a picture. Sometimes the colours in a scene can make a picture in themselves – in autumn, for example, when reds, browns and golds make a stunning sight of trees which you would not usually notice – but too many bright and jarring colours will confuse the eye in just the same way as a jumbled subject does. In a particularly colourful scene, try to pick out one or two bright colours and surround them with more subtle tones, rather than snapping a whole range of different ones. Look out for attractive pastel shades. If you can, choose colours which lend themselves to the mood of the picture – in picking a background, for example. There is no point in taking colour pictures unless the colours are attractive and go together well.

Indoor Lighting – Available Light

Available light is the name given to rather dim natural light, such as that coming into a room through a window. It also refers to poor natural light out of doors; at dusk or on a very dull day, for example. Available light is an effective way of lighting a subject and can be better than using flash, particularly if an ultra-fast film is used. The drawback is that there is sometimes not enough light to take a picture without help from flash or artificial lighting.

Choose a sunny day and take some light readings indoors. You can alter the ASA setting on your camera or light meter to see what difference a faster film would make. Try taking readings from objects on a windowsill or near the window, in direct light and in shadow. Then go further

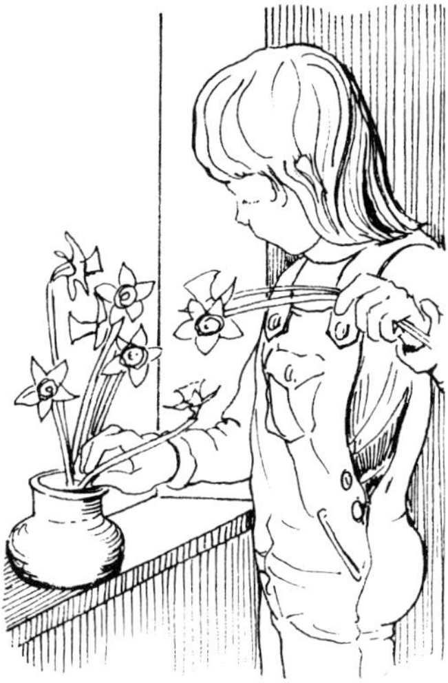

Always check how the lighting falls

into the room and see what the difference is. Remember that you must use a speed of 1/60 or more, unless you have a tripod, or can rest your camera on a firm surface.

Under most conditions, you will find that you get the best results if the subject is near the window, particularly if the picture is a portrait with sunlight as part of the composition. Ask a friend to sit near a window, and study the effect of the sun at different angles. If he sits with his back to the window, his face will be silhouetted, but if he sits sideways at the window, so that the light is shining on one side of his face, the effect can be interesting. Ask him to turn his head slightly and see how the shadows fall.

A possible disadvantage of side lighting is that one side of the subject's face will be brightly lit while the other is in shadow. You can highlight the shadowed side by asking a friend to hold up a sheet of white card or a white sheet inside the room to bounce the light back on to the subject, thus lightening the shadows.

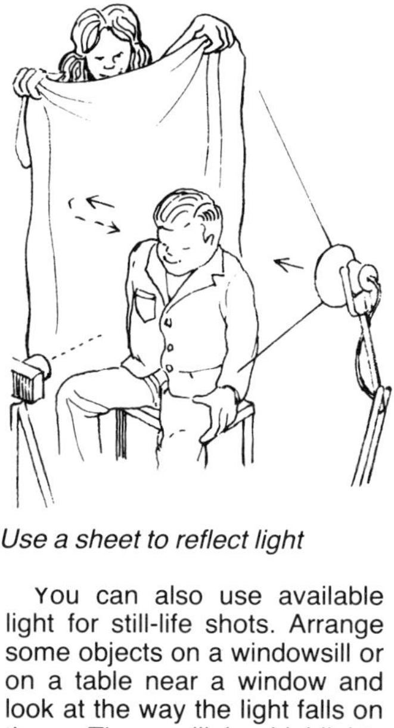

Use a sheet to reflect light

You can also use available light for still-life shots. Arrange some objects on a windowsill or on a table near a window and look at the way the light falls on them. There will be highlights and shadows, and the effect will be more subtle than the harsher light you would get with flash.

Artificial Light

If you take colour pictures using only the artificial electric lighting in a room – they will have an orange tint. This can be effective for some subjects, but not for others. If you use flash, the bright light overrides the less powerful room lights so the colours will be more natural. It is possible to take colour pictures in artificial light alone, using a tungsten film, or with ordinary daylight film, using a blue filter to counteract the orange light.

Artificial light is no problem with black and white photographs.

Using Flash

Flash helps you to take pictures in any light conditions. You can use it as the only source of light or to fill in poor available light and highlight a subject.

There are various types of flash attachment, and you can check which to use with your camera by asking a photographic dealer. Some cameras have a built-in flash. Others take a flash bulb or bar of bulbs, or a flash cube. If your camera doesn't have a built-in flash, it will have a flash shoe for fitting a flash attachment.

Read the instructions with your camera to find out how a built-in flash works. With a

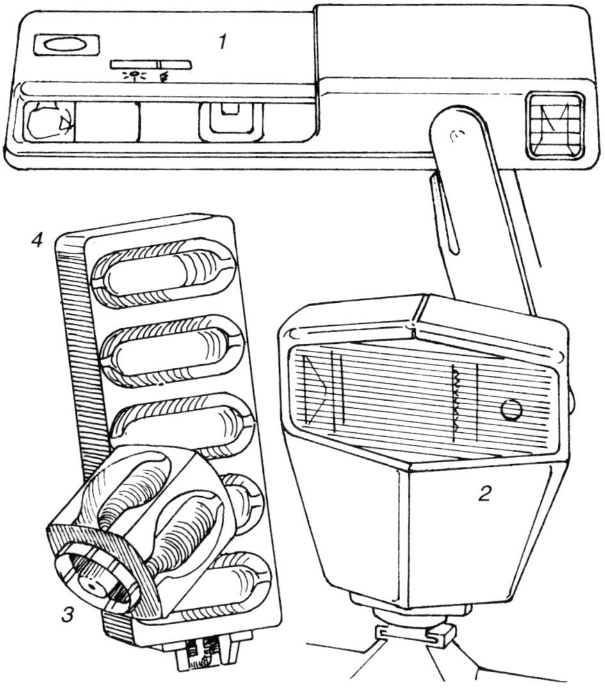

1 Built-in flash

2 Flash gun

3 Flash cube

4 Flash bar

simple camera, for example, it is normally just a matter of switching the camera to the flash setting and taking the picture. The flash runs on batteries and you must check from time to time that these are not wearing out, as the flash will not work properly if they are.

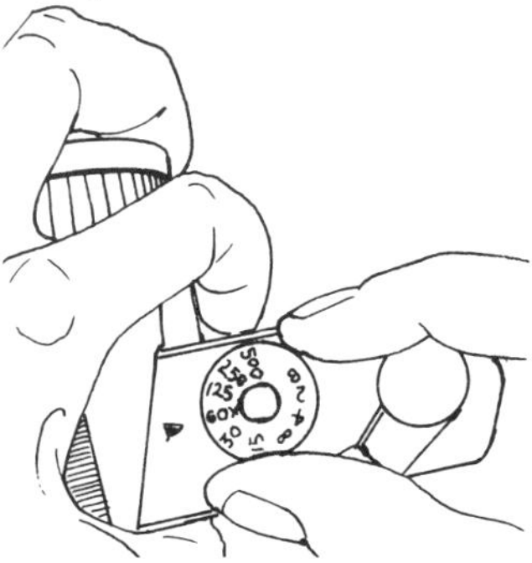

X setting on a camera

A flash cube has four bulbs and tiny reflectors, so can be used four times before it is thrown away. The cube is turned round after each shot until all four bulbs have been used.

The most versatile sort of flash unit is a separate flash gun. Some flash guns are not adjustable. You fit them on the flash shoe and they shine straight at the subject. This will give you a picture, of course, but you can get more interesting effects if the angle of the flash can be altered. Some guns, for example, have a swivel head so that you can point the light up at the ceiling or at a wall to bounce back on to the subject. Sometimes you can take the flash off the camera on an extension lead. Flash guns use batteries which, again, should be checked.

Flash guns work in different ways, but most cameras have a flash setting, normally marked with an X. This sets the shutter speed and fires the flash automatically when you take the picture. The flash gun may have a range of settings for altering the flash distance from the subject, and this tells you which aperture to set on the camera. With others, you calculate the exposure by a GUIDE NUMBER system. The guide number is given on the flash gun and you divide it by the distance from the subject to find the correct f-number. Read the instructions that come with your camera and with the flash gun and make sure you know how to use them together.

Using flash is not complicated once you understand how your particular flash attachment works, but there are some points to remember.

On simple flash guns, you cannot alter the distance, and these only light up a short area, normally between 1.5 and 3 metres, so it is important to make sure that your subject is within this range. If the subject is any closer, it will be over-exposed and look washed-out. If the subject is further away, it will come out too dark.

A fixed flash, shining directly on the subject, gives a rather harsh light, and people's eyes will come out red if they are looking at the camera. So, if you can avoid it, don't have people looking at the flash.

If your flash can be set for different distances, carefully estimate the distance to your subject and notice what else will

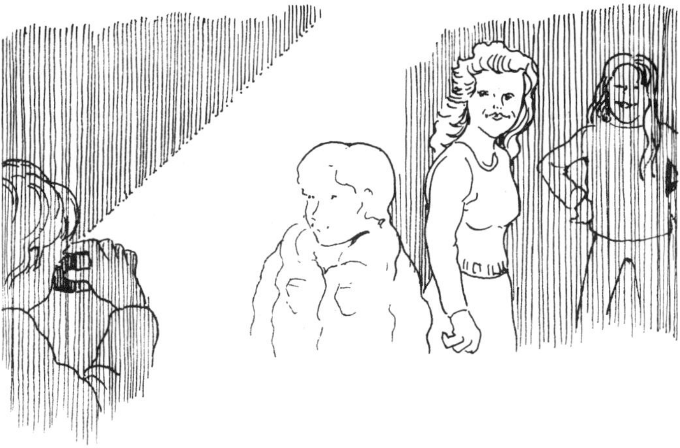

Too close and the subject is over-exposed; outside the flash the subject is under-exposed. The girl in the centre is correctly positioned

be within the range of the flash. Choose the most suitable aperture for the picture you want.

Be careful about reflections. Don't point the flash towards a mirror, window, picture glass, or any highly polished surface or you will get a reflection in the picture.

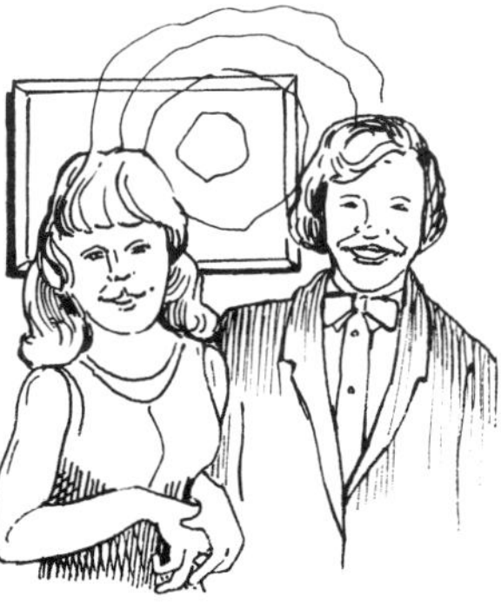

Beware of reflections

BOUNCE FLASH

If you use direct flash – that is, where the flash is shining straight at the subject – the light will be flat and harsh. There will also be ugly shadows if the background is too close to the subject. (This can be avoided, of course, by moving the subject away from the background.) You can't see the effect of the flash beforehand, as you can with other types of lighting, so there may be some very disappointing results.

As a general rule, direct flash is fine for quick photrographs, such as shots at parties, but if you are taking a flash portrait, and your flash gun allows this, it is usually better to bounce the flash off a light-coloured ceiling or wall. To do this, you point the flash so that the light shines up at the ceiling or on to a wall above the subject, remembering to increase the distance setting on the flash gun. The light bounces

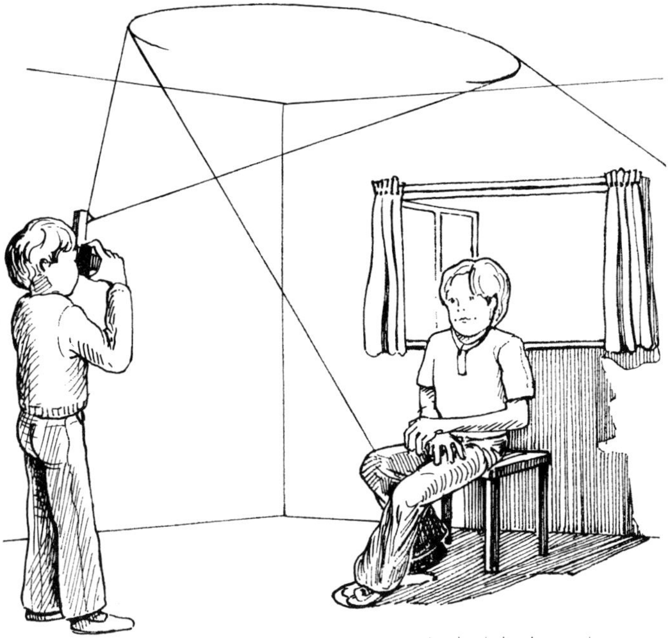

Bouncing flash off the ceiling

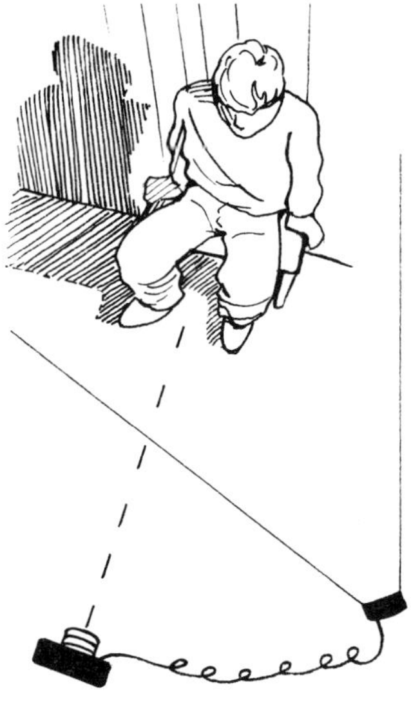

Using an extension lead

off this surface and is reflected back on to the subject. This gives a softer, more interesting effect. Beware of coloured walls or ceilings – the colour may tinge the light reflected back on to the subject.

If you have a flash gun which can be moved away from the camera on an extension lead, you can direct the light even more carefully, to avoid harsh shadows and get the effect you want. Using off-camera flash also avoids red-eye in pictures of people.

FILL-IN FLASH

As well as being a complete light source, flash can also be used to fill in dark parts of an available light picture. For example, you may want to put a subject with his back to a window because you like the overall composition, but his face is in shadow, which spoils the picture. If you use flash as well, this lights up the subject's face, so that you have the best of both worlds.

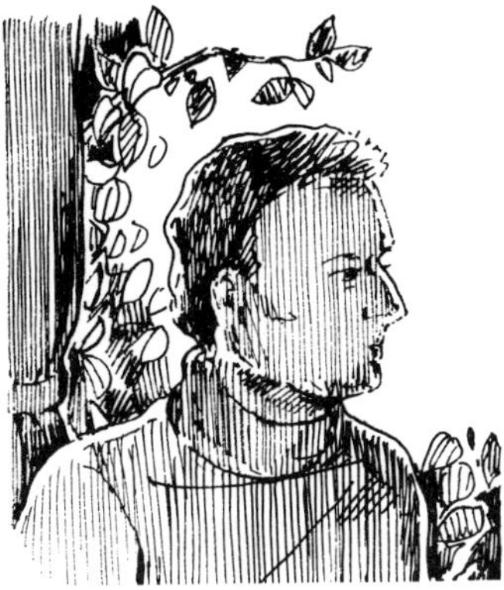

Use daylight and flash together to achieve the best effect

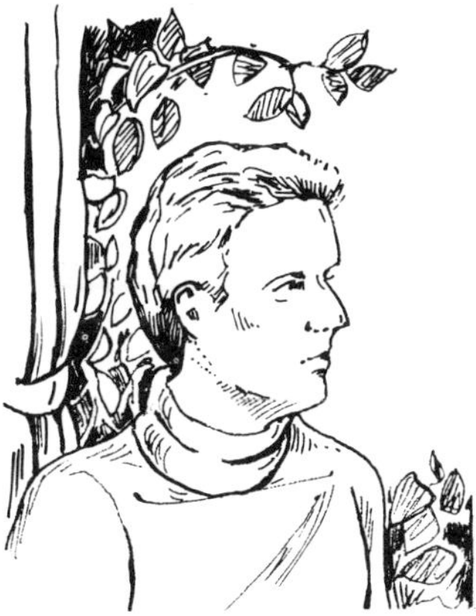

To use fill-in flash, you need to make a simple exposure calculation so that the daylight and flashlight work together. First take an exposure reading for the scene without flash, and match it with the speed of your flash setting. Suppose your flash setting is 1/60 and the exposure for this speed is f/8. Check the distance scale, or calculate the distance by the guide number method (this time divide the guide number by the f-number) to see what range you have at this aperture, and make sure your subject is within it.

Sometimes it is a good idea to reduce the aperture setting by one stop from that suggested by the light meter; for example, if it is a bright day and you think the daylight and flash together may make the picture over-exposed. You can only learn this by experiment. Practise fill-in flash techniques and take some pairs of pictures, with and without flash, so that you can study the different effects.

USING FLASH OUT OF DOORS

You can produce extra light in dim conditions by using flash out of doors. If it is a dull day, you can use fill-in flash to highlight the subject against a darker background. Take a light reading of the scene, check your flash setting, and reduce the exposure by one stop, if necessary. Flash will even work well out of doors at night, to light subjects at a bonfire party, for example.

Practise using flash in all these different ways, if only to see the effects it produces. The thought of flash may be worrying

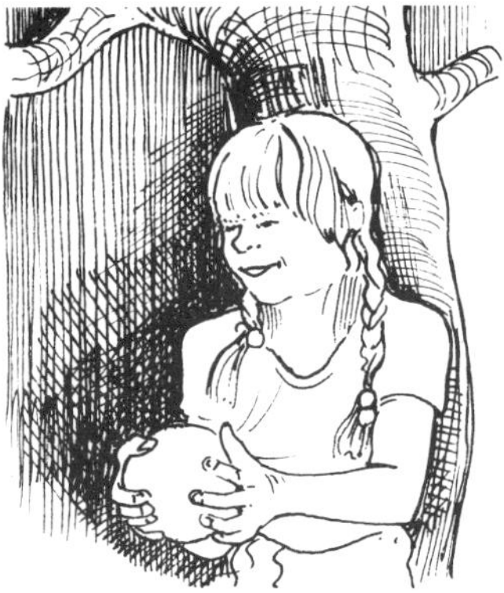

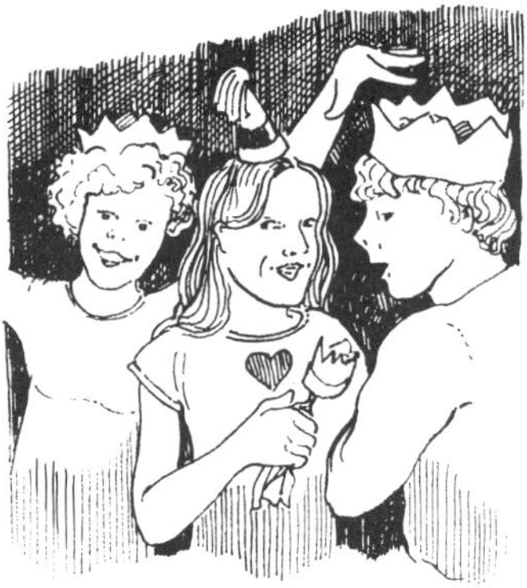

You can use flash out of doors on a dull day or at a night-time party

because there is no way of seeing the effect except by taking a picture, but practice will soon help you to imagine what the result will be. The main thing, whatever type of camera and flash you have, is to make sure that the flash light reaches the subject and that it works together with the controls on the camera.

A composition of light and shade

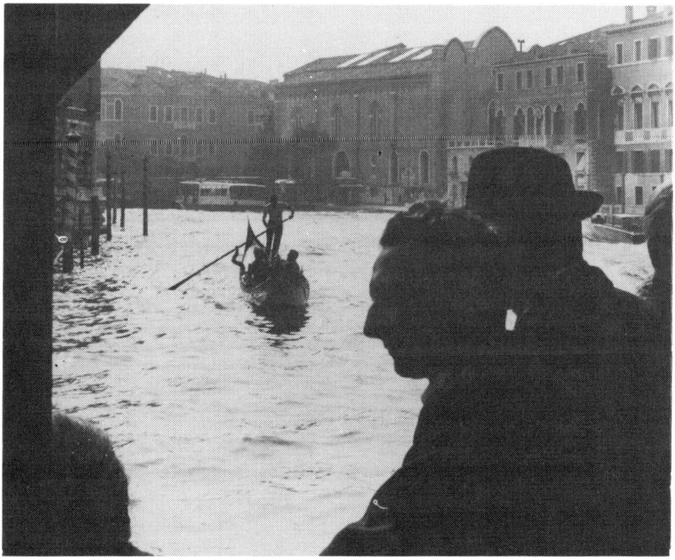

CHAPTER 8

Looking for Pictures

When you first use your camera, you will probably take pictures of anything and everything, just to see how they come out. You will gradually become more selective, and begin to reject ideas that do not please you when you study them in the viewfinder.

Learning to look for pictures and to recognise what will make a good composition is something that you can only pick up by trying things out. If you take plenty of pictures, you can study the results carefully to see what looks good, where you are going wrong, and what you should do next time. Thumb through some photography books and decide which pictures you like, and which you don't like. Then try to work out what it is that you particularly like or dislike about them.

Some people spend the whole year without taking a single picture, and then expect to produce film after film of perfect shots when they go on holiday, or on a special occasion. They are often disappointed, for two main reasons. Firstly, it is important to practise everything thoroughly so that you can use the controls of your camera without thinking when you need to; and secondly, looking for and finding the best pictures needs to be learnt like any other skill.

Pictures are all around you all the time, not just in holiday resorts or on special occasions. If you look at other people's photographs, you will see that many of the most successful are of very ordinary subjects. The photographer has seen something in a person's face, or a street of houses, or the pattern of fields, perhaps, and it appealed to him. Would you have seen the same things? Probably not, if you hadn't trained yourself to look for them. At first it is easy to walk past a whole film's worth of pictures without even thinking of getting your camera out.

You can look for pictures at any time, even when you haven't got a camera with you. Make a viewing frame with your thumbs and index fingers and practise framing possible pictures around your house, street or town. If you have your camera, compose lots of different pictures in the viewfinder, without actually taking any, and reject those which don't completely please you.

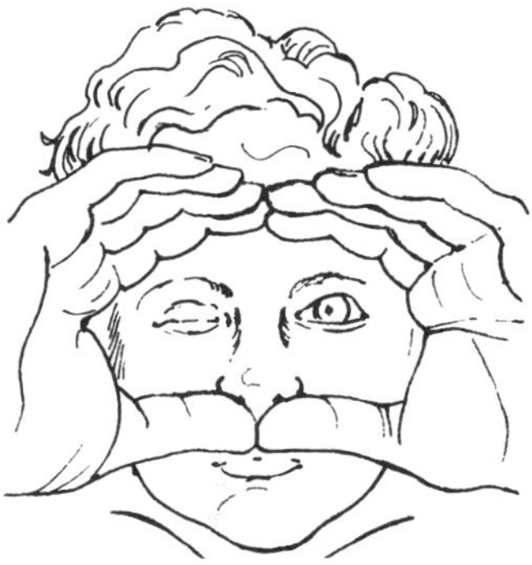

Make a frame with your hands

In Town

As you walk down a street, look at anything and everything to decide whether it would make a picture. Then try framing each idea, with your fingers or the

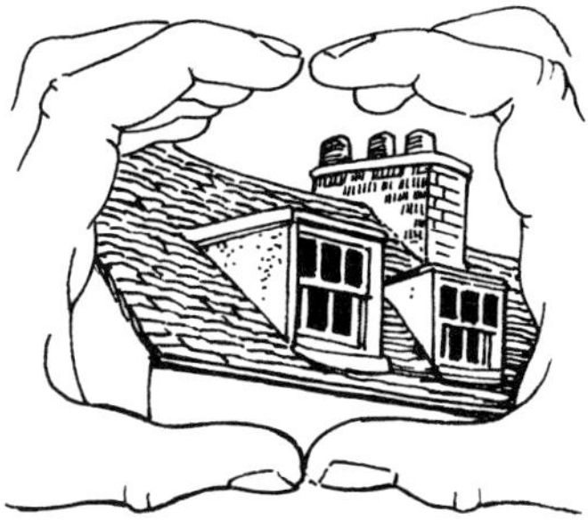

Use your hands as a frame to pick out a detail

camera viewfinder, to see if you were right. In a town, look beyond the obvious to individual details on buildings, for example. Look for patterns made by doorways or windows, rooftops or chimneys. Shop windows, signs or posters can make pictures. Small splashes of colour, such as window boxes, tubs or hanging baskets are attractive, and of course there are flower pictures to be found in gardens or parks. Look for interesting pictures of people (but make sure they don't mind being photographed first). Practise getting very close to a subject to cut out all the surrounding bits and pieces, and try to notice things that would spoil a picture – drainpipes, television aerials, road signs – so that you don't overlook them when it is a picture that really matters.

Look for pictures that show the character of a place (historic buildings in an old town; soaring skyscrapers in a new town). On old buildings, look for details like gables and gargoyles that might make pictures in themselves.

Keep an eye open, too, for interesting glimpses of views – through a doorway, at the end of an alleyway, or between trees. Try to avoid an obvious picture unless you merely want a record shot.

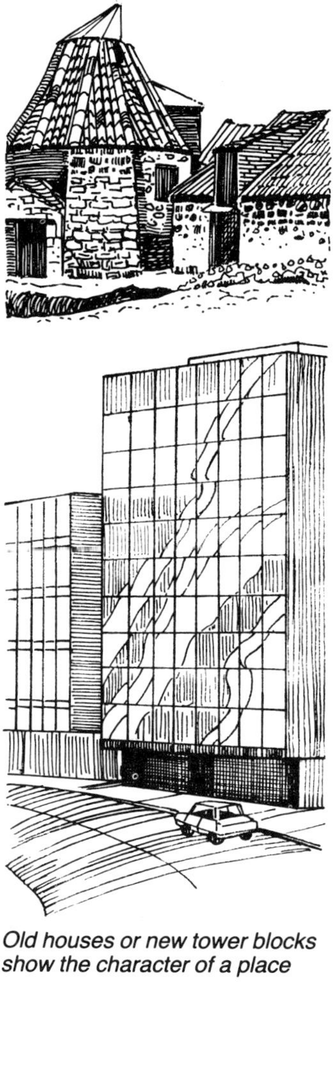

Old houses or new tower blocks show the character of a place

Sometimes you will see a picture that tells a story. A bicycle leaning against a doorway might suggest an idea. Where is its owner? Where does the doorway lead? Footprints in the snow, or a glimpse into a house through an open doorway may have the same effect.

If you are using colour film, pictures can be made with colour and very little else. Sometimes a combination of colour and texture will make a good shot – peeling paintwork, rust, moss-covered tiles, the petals of a flower, perhaps. Bold colours can also be effective as a subject – vegetables or flowers on a market stall, for example, side-shows at a fairground, toys or sticks of rock in a seaside gift shop. With black and white shots, look for contrasts, bold shapes, textures, and interesting skies. Try to imagine subjects without their colour. Would they be less interesting?

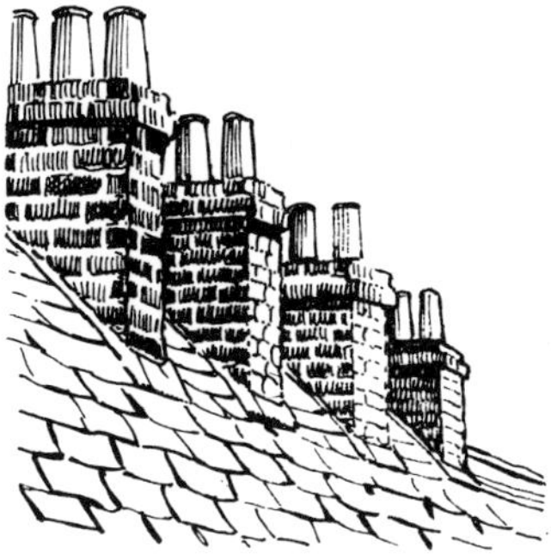

Rooftops can make a good pattern picture

Seeing pictures is quite an individual thing. Something which appeals to you may not appeal to your friend. This doesn't mean it is wrong. If a picture pleases you, then it is worth taking.

As a first stage in training yourself to look for pictures, try walking down a street in your town and see if you can spot twenty possible subjects that you like the look of. You may find more than twenty, or you may not find as many that really appeal to you. That isn't the point. The point is learning to look.

Keep a Note of It

It is a good idea to carry your notebook and pencil with you, particularly in the early stages. As well as noting down exposures and other technical details as you take a picture, you can jot down possible places of interest and subjects to come back to, and make a note of where you took each picture. It is surprising how easy it is to forget the details, especially if the film is in the camera for some time. Sometimes it might be worth coming back to a subject at a different time of day, or even at a different season of the year. If you take sets of pictures for comparison – different lighting shots, for example, or the same subject from different viewpoints – make a note of all the details so that you really can compare them. There is not much point in knowing that one looks better than another if you can't remember what you did in either case!

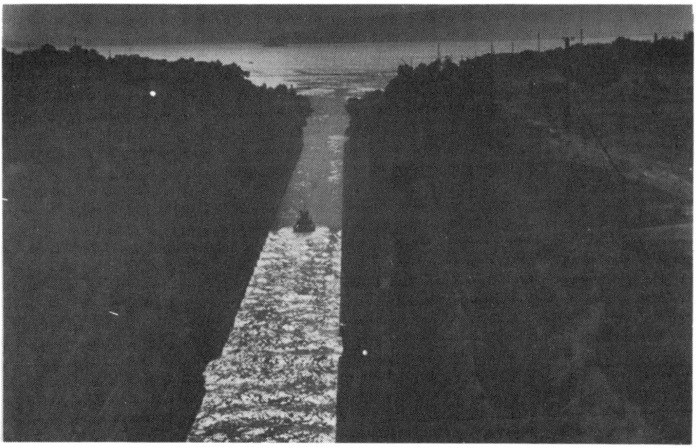

Country Walks

In the countryside, look for patterns of leaves and branches, patchwork quilts of fields, and interesting combinations of colour and texture as well as landscape views. Try different viewpoints. Climb a hill and take the scene spread out below, or lie flat on your stomach for pictures of flowers and plants.

A country village may have a pond with ducks and other water birds on it, or you may come across a river. Experiment with different ways of capturing moving water. You may want to photograph a stream rushing over stones, or a waterfall. A fast shutter speed will 'freeze' the water in its tracks, but sometimes it is better to choose a slower shutter speed and have everything sharp except the water. The blur creates an effect of swirling movement.

Don't be so captivated by a busy river that you forget the foreground. A picture will be spoilt by a boring expanse of empty water in front of the first boat or water bird. Look for boats

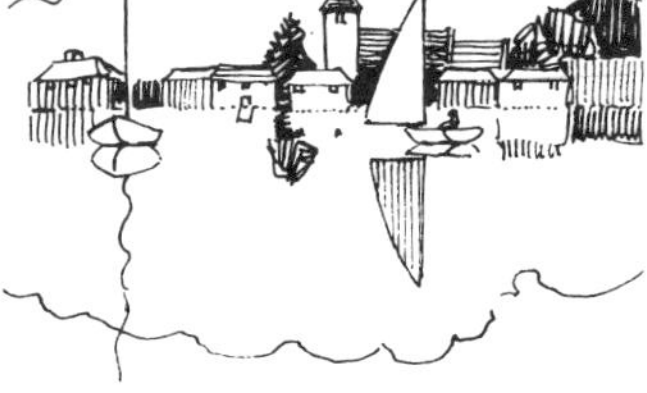

An empty foreground is boring

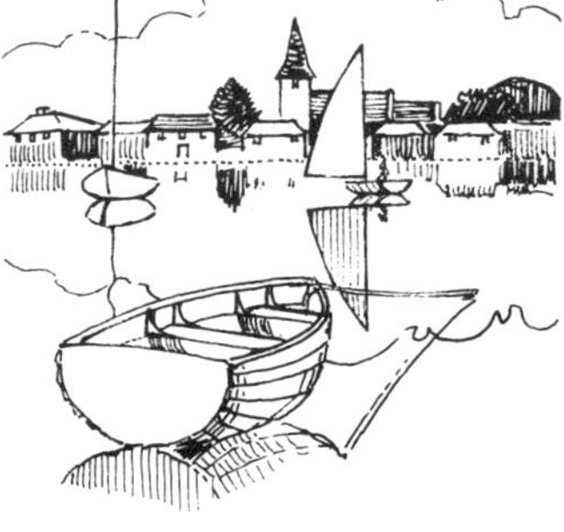

moored at the bank, or trees or shrubs to fill the foreground, or wait until water birds come near the bank, and get down low to frame the picture.

A calm river or lake may have mirror images of bridges, buildings or overhanging trees reflected in it. Choose a time

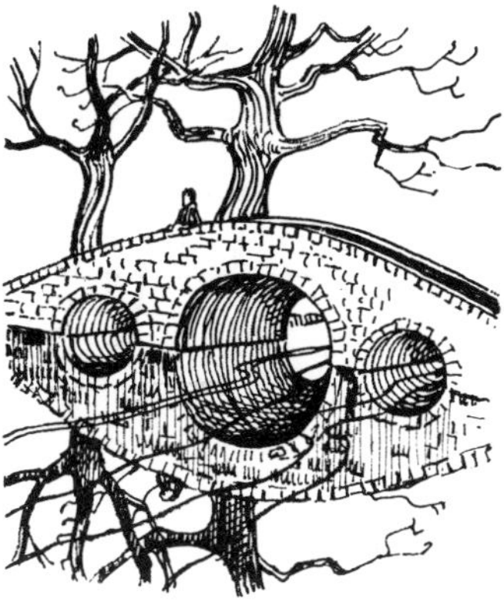

Finding a mirror image

when the sun is not shining directly on the water, or use a polarising filter to cut out the glare of the light on the water and little points of light which may spoil the reflection. For a perfect mirror image, the water must be completely calm, with barely a ripple on it. Frame the picture so that both halves – image and reflection – are as nearly identical as you can make them.

Look for items of interest that would set off a pleasant view. Farm machinery, a weathered old barn, hay bales, or animals in a field could provide foreground interest. A tractor or combine harvester in a field may be enough to change an otherwise ordinary scene. Fences and gates can be used for framing, as a focal point, or to lead the eye into the scene. A copse of trees may add some height to a flat landscape. A cottage or a mellow old wall may be eye-catchers in the scene. Look, too, for bold lines – hills and crags are more interesting than a flat skyline.

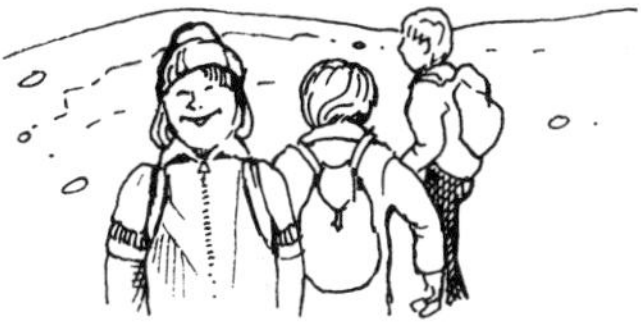

This picture is rather flat and dull

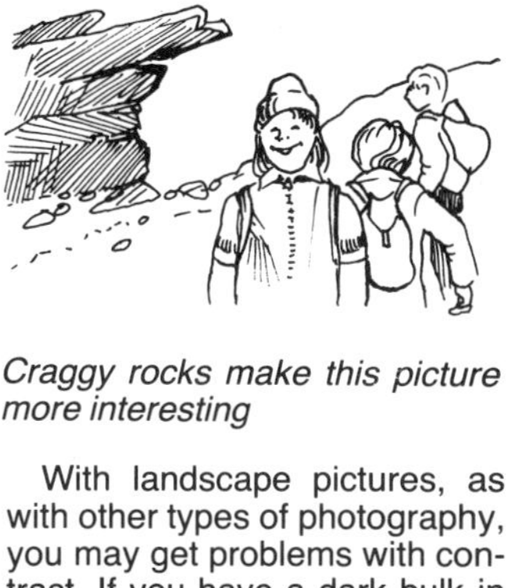

Craggy rocks make this picture more interesting

With landscape pictures, as with other types of photography, you may get problems with contrast. If you have a dark bulk in the foreground, such as a barn or a piece of machinery, and a bright scene behind, a general exposure reading would probably make the dark foreground look under-exposed. Taking a reading from the dark part only would make the rest of the picture come out over-exposed. If you are worried about contrast, it is

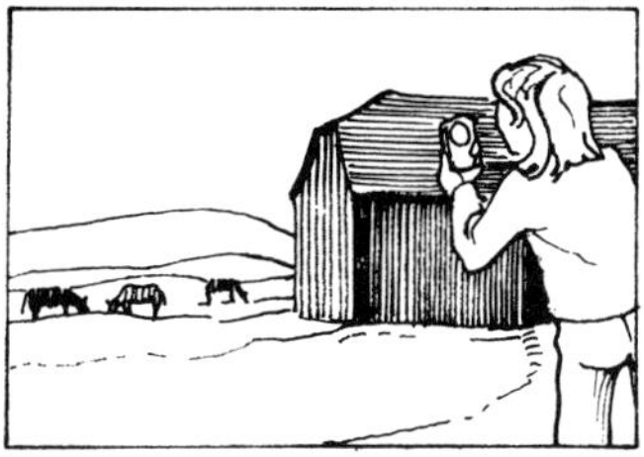

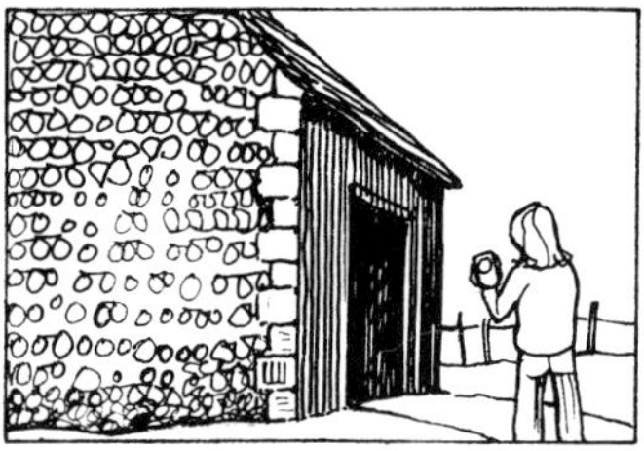

Take plenty of light readings to get the best results

usually best to choose a setting between the two, or you could BRACKET exposures if you want to make sure that the picture will be all right. To do this, take one picture at the chosen exposure setting, then take another at one f-stop more, and a third at one f-stop less. You use more film this way, but there is more chance of getting the best setting. Another method is to choose a part of the scene which you think is about halfway between the darkest and the lightest bits, and take a reading from that.

If you have a polarising filter, use it for landscape shots on a bright day. It will reduce glare and give you a clear blue sky rather than the washed-out white that might result if there are contrast problems.

Experiment with different lenses, if you have them. A wide-angle is useful for taking in a wider view, not just of a distant landscape, but of closer subjects like a spreading tree or a line of trees which you couldn't fit into the frame with a standard lens. A telephoto, of course, can be used to pull in a distant part of the view; for example, if you want to bring a distant building or village closer, and cut out uninteresting foreground altogether.

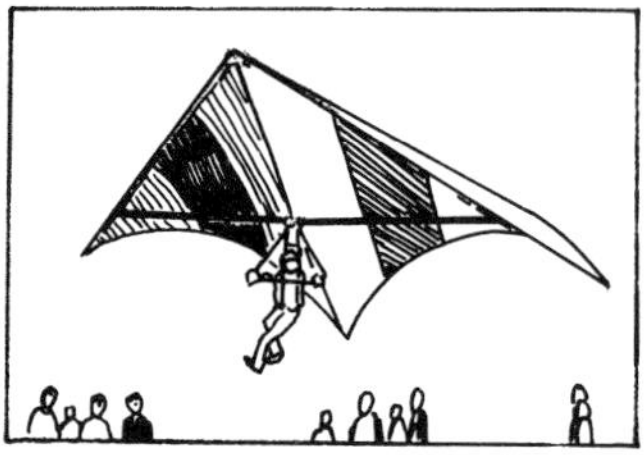

Standard lens

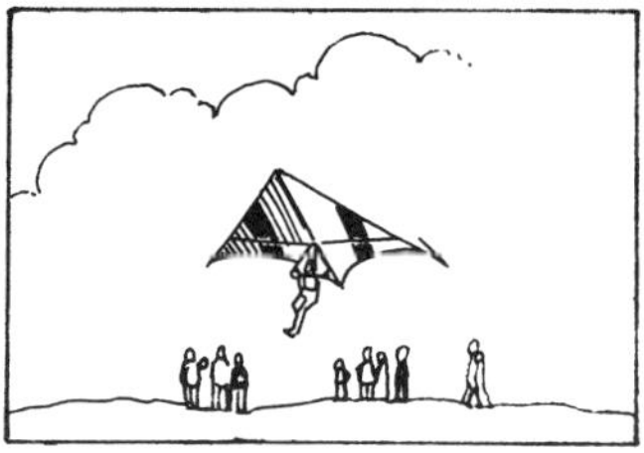

Wide-angle lens

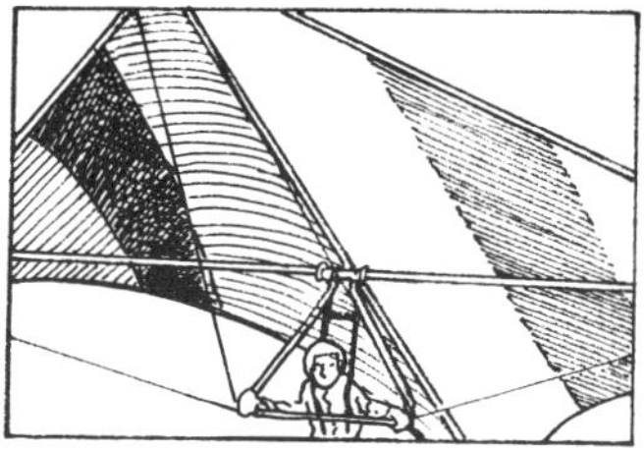

Telephoto lens

If you want a PANORAMA picture (a wide view) and you haven't a wide-angle lens, you can take a series of pictures with your standard lens and stick them together. Make sure that each picture slightly overlaps with the next and that there are points you can recognise for matching up the prints. To join the pictures together, line them up carefully, cut off the overlapping bit and stick the panorama on to a piece of card.

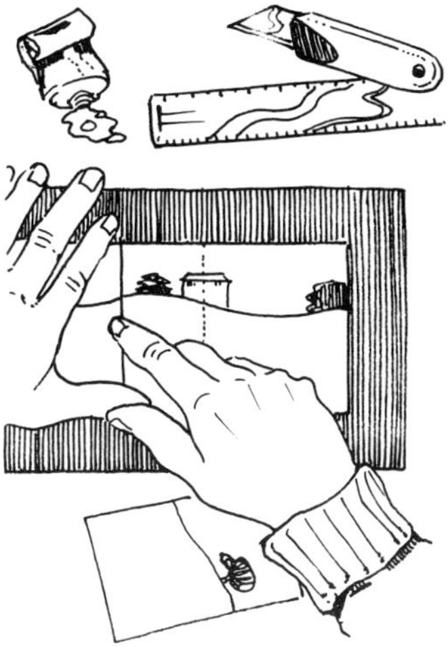

Creating a panorama picture

Look for pictures of people in the countryside, too: a family feeding the ducks, perhaps; a farmer driving a tractor, or leading a herd of animals from one field to another; people messing about in boats; fishermen; walkers; or people just dozing in the sun. Keep an eye open for village markets, craft fairs and fetes with photographic possibilities.

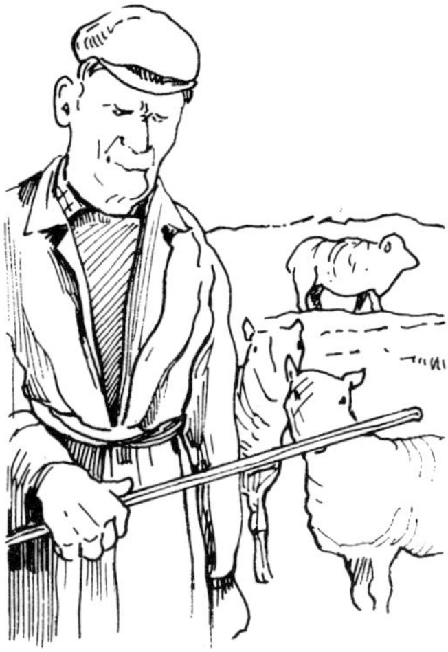

An interesting personality adds character to your picture

Remember to look out for details too. Flowers growing on old stone walls, mossy stones and tiles, and plants growing in hidden corners of woods can make good subjects, as can close-ups of tree bark, recently cut tree stumps, or gnarled tree roots.

The Seasons

The seasons of the year have plenty to offer the photographer. Apart from the more obvious things like the foliage of the trees, and the plant and animal life, there are very different sorts of skies, colours and moods to be captured on film.

It is an interesting exercise to take pictures of the same tree or copse of trees at different times of the year. In the winter, the tree branches are bare and stark, and their shapes against the sky

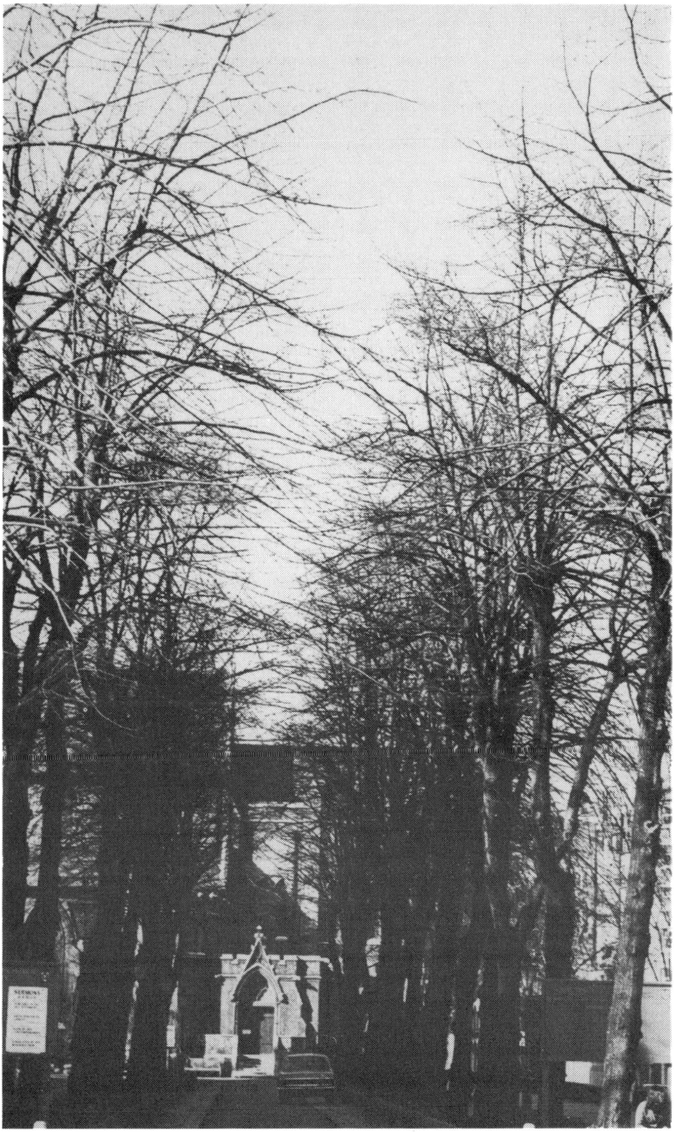

Trees outlined against the sky

make the picture. Sometimes a winter picture of a tree looks effective in silhouette against the sun to emphasise the shape of the branches. In the spring the tree has young green leaves, and maybe blossom. In the summer it is full-blown – try to take it on a typical summer's day, against a blue sky – and the autumn, of course, is the time of red, brown and yellow tints which make photographs worth taking for the colour alone.

Winter can be illustrated by stormy skies and snow scenes. If you are using black and white film, remember to put a yellow or orange filter on the lens to make the clouds stronger. Try to choose a scene which matches the sky – perhaps a bleak, lonely landscape, with twisted old trees and gathering storm clouds above.

Sunlight on a snow scene can cause problems, because light is reflected from the snow. If you take an exposure reading by pointing the meter at a bright snow scene, the meter will suggest a high reading because of the glare from the snow. This will make other parts of the picture, such as buildings, people and trees, look under-exposed. If you can, take a reading from something in the foreground and choose a setting between the two, or allow one stop more exposure than the overall reading suggests.

You can take happy scenes on bright blue days, with snow sparkling on trees and roof-tops, and people tobogganning, throwing snowballs or making snowmen.

Snow on bare branches, ledges, rooftops and windowsills makes new shapes and patterns. Footprints and car tracks in fresh snow give pattern pictures, as do frost and ice on window panes or the edges of a roof. Everything looks different after a new fall of snow. There must be shapes in the scene to make up for the lack of colour, or perhaps people in bright clothes against the snow. You could take landscape pictures, showing the contrast between snowy fields and dark trees, or use fences, gates or walls to make patterns against the snow.

In spring, the fresh greens and delicate shades of the newly-opened flowers are worth capturing. There are blossoms and banks of primroses, and young lambs in the fields. Make sure you get close enough to your subject to make a picture – take a spray of blossom rather than a distant tree; and a close-up of one or two primroses rather than several faraway dots.

In summer, look for bright, hot colours under blue cloud-less skies (remember to use a polarising filter, if you have one) – fields of ripening corn, summer flowers and woodland scenes with vivid green leaves, all make good summer pictures. Reds and yellows illustrate summer well.

In autumn, woods or wooded landscapes are the best places to capture all the different colours, but heathland can be beautiful, too, with its golden bracken and shrubs. Wait for clear days when the sun really brings out the colours, and look out for bright berries to add even more colour to a scene.

Seascapes

If you live near the sea, or go to the coast for your holidays, you have another ready-made subject to work with. The sea itself offers a host of different types of picture – stormy, rough weather scenes with waves crashing against rocks or cliffs, views of calm blue water with tiny lacy waves breaking on the beach, and all the moods and colours in between. The landscape of the coast, with cliffs, beaches, rocks, seaside towns and harbours, also gives plenty of scope.

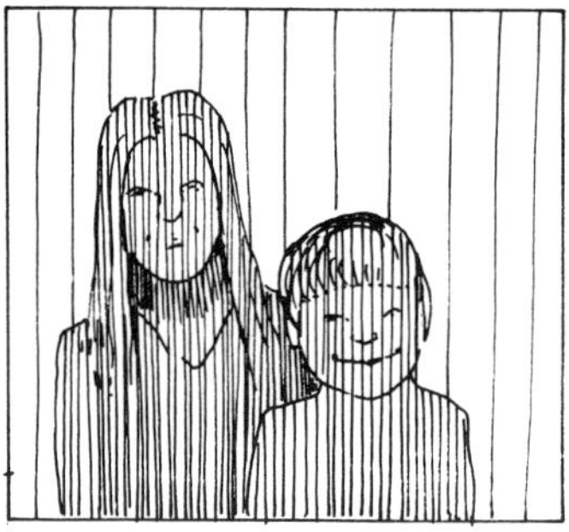

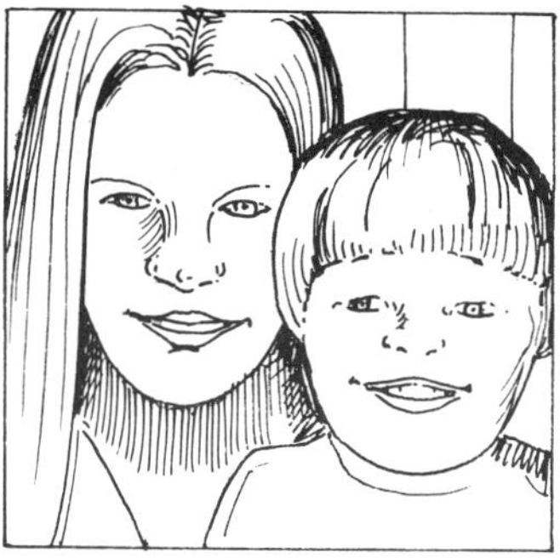

Moving closer cuts out glare

There are exposure problems near the sea because of reflected light. The sea and light-coloured sand reflect light, and this can result in over-exposure, so choose a small aperture, or keep your camera on the 'sunny' setting for seaside pictures even if the weather is cloudy. If you are taking a picture of a subject against a background of sea and sand – people on the beach, for example – the subject will be under-exposed if you take a reading for sea and sky. Take a reading from the subject as well, if you can, or allow one stop more exposure than for the general scene. Then cut out some of the glaring surroundings by moving in close to the subject.

Into-the-sun pictures can be effective by the sea, particularly at sunset. Try to get the light on the edges of the waves, and have something in silhouette in the foreground – a boat or a person, for example.

You will need a fast shutter speed to 'freeze' waves crashing on to the beach or against a cliff or pier. Try to catch the moment when the surf shoots high in the air or the biggest wave breaks on to the beach.

Rather like landscapes, seascapes do not usually succeed unless there is something else in the picture besides the sea. Try to include a rock or breakwater, a cliff or a boat, or people walking, fishing, or throwing stones into the water. Remember to think about the horizon, and make sure it is either above or below the centre of the picture.

Tracks on the sand, coloured stones and seaweeds all make subjects for pattern pictures.

You need sunlight to add shape and shadow. Study the effect when the sun is shining on the subject at different angles. The colours of stones show up best when the sun is not too bright, as very bright sun adds glare.

You can take pictures of rock pools with a polarising filter to cut out the reflection of the sky on the water, or by choosing a pool that is shaded from the sunlight. Don't point the camera straight down at the water – an angle of about 45° is best.

In a seaside town, go to the harbour for colourful shots of fishing boats and nets, fishermen and general bustle. Look for interesting patterns made by masts, or a row of differently coloured boats moored together. There may be reflection pictures in a calm harbour. Avoid taking general muddly scenes, and choose one subject to create the atmosphere you want.

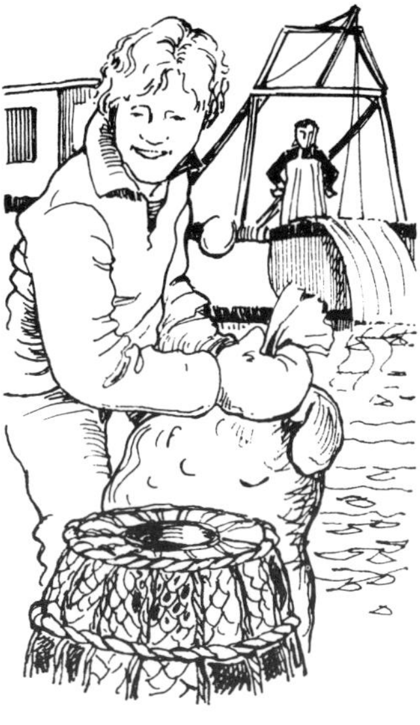

Look for people at work

The town may have a fairground or some outdoor amusements which provide cheerful subjects. Look for colour and action in this type of picture – colourful stalls, roundabouts and other rides (choose a fast shutter speed if they are moving – see page 8), and people enjoying themselves. Again, pick a theme rather than a general scene.

If you have telephoto and close-up lenses, you can experiment with pictures of seabirds, flowers growing on cliffs, shellfish on the rocks, crabs in the sand, and all the wildlife of the seaside.

When you are taking pictures near the sea, remember that sand and salt water can damage your camera. Put the camera back in its case with the lens cap on when you are not using it, and keep a UV or skylight filter on the lens all the time. Don't put your camera down on the sand.

The Sky

The weather affects all outdoor photography – whether the sun is shining, what colour the sky is and so on – but you can take pictures of the weather, too. The sky is an interesting subject, particularly if there are spectacular clouds, and it is also possible to take pictures of rain, rainbows, sunsets, or mist.

If you are using your camera in wet weather, make sure that it is properly protected. Keep it in a case or a plastic bag when you are not taking pictures, and leave a UV or skylight filter on the lens all the time.

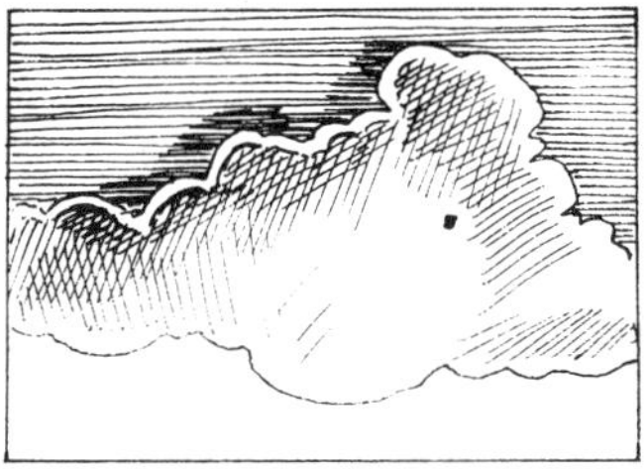

Clouds create dramatic pictures

Remember that clouds will look even more dramatic on black and white film if you use a yellow, orange or red filter to increase the contrast. Keep the horizon low, so that the sky dominates as the main subject, and try to choose a suitable landscape for the cloud effects. You might take a picture with no horizon at all, concentrating solely on the sky. This looks effective if there is a large bank of dark cloud with some light shining through, for example.

Use colour film to photograph a rainbow against a dark sky, so that the colours show up well. Either colour or black and white film can be used for pictures of mist and fog, though black and white is often more effective. If you are using colour film, choose scenes with soft colours to fit in with the mood you are trying to capture. Find some solid shapes that stand out against the mist – buildings, people, trees – to give the picture some point. Sometimes you can get interesting and eerie effects with combinations of light and mist – when the sun is trying to break through, for example, or when mist is hanging round street lights. You may need long exposures if the mist is thick, so use a tripod or rest your camera on a steady surface.

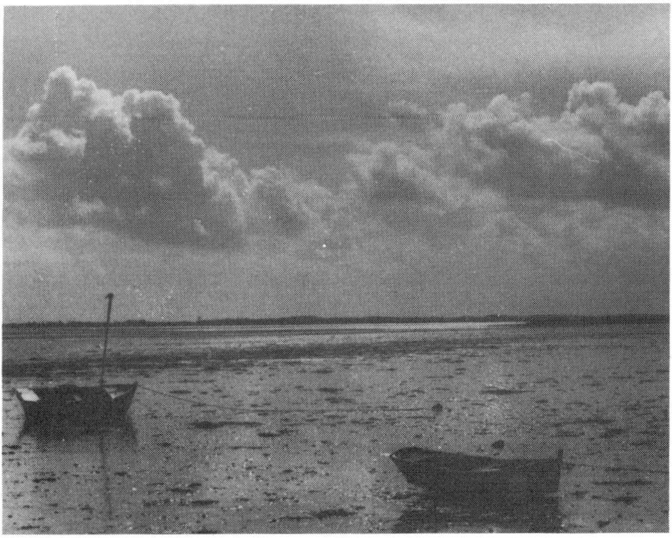

Though you can't take a picture of rain falling, you can catch raindrops as they land, or when they are running down a surface, such as a window. Raindrops plopping into puddles may make a good picture, for instance. Look for the glistening scenes just after a fall of rain, with puddles and wet surfaces which reflect the light. Include people with bright macs and umbrellas, perhaps, for added interest. Black and white pictures of rainy conditions, with heavy skies and dark tones, are very effective. (Remember that water on the lens will come out in the picture, so stand in some shelter to take your pictures.)

Sunsets are ideal subjects for into-the-light shots, with surrounding objects shown in silhouette, because the sun will not be bright enough to dazzle. Seascapes with the sun setting look good, and so do people walking along a skyline against the setting sun.

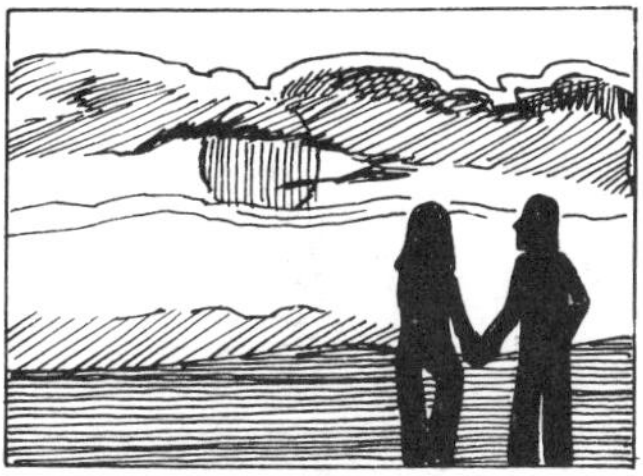

Into-the-light picture

Plan your picture so that you catch the sun at the crucial moment before it gets too dark and starts to disappear. The sky will have all sorts of pink and orange lights which will add to the effect, particularly if there are some interesting clouds around.

Taking Pictures at Night

You need an adjustable camera to take pictures at night because the shutter has to stay open for far longer than a basic camera will allow. You also need a firm surface or tripod to rest your camera on.

Most adjustable cameras have a 'B' setting on the shutter speed dial. When you set this and press the shutter release, the shutter stays open until you let the shutter release go, so you can take pictures in dim conditions and still get a result.

Use a fast film for night photography, so that you don't have to keep the shutter open for any longer than is absolutely necessary. The most effective night shots are those where there are plenty of bright lights, such as in the centre of a big city. Choose a spot where you can rest your camera on a wall or railings if you haven't a tripod, and take some light readings. You might find you have to leave the shutter open for complete seconds to

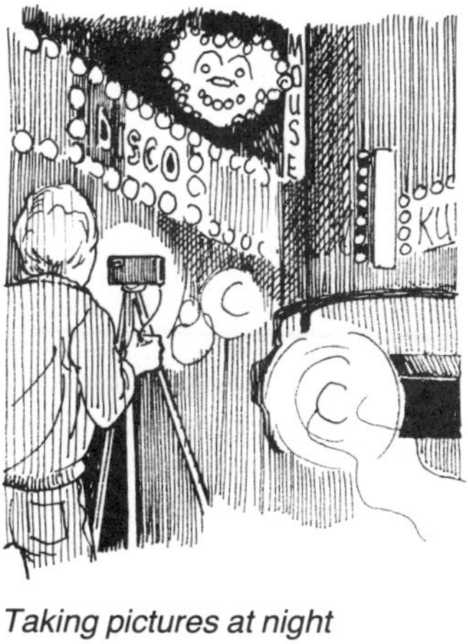

Taking pictures at night

get a picture. You can use a large aperture, of course, but this may not give you enough depth of field for the pictures you want.

The headlights on moving cars will come out as long streaks of light on the picture. This is because the shutter is open for so long that the car has time to move right across the frame and its image is photographed for the whole distance. Car lights make interesting pictures, particularly if you include red tail-lights. In the heart of a big city, you can take a picture that is made up entirely of lights – car lights, street lights, lighted windows, large neon signs – and there is so much dazzle that you can see people wandering about and the buildings around them. You will need slow shutter speeds, even where the scene looks almost as bright as day.

This is one sort of night shot, but there are others. A single building, or a tree under a full moon can look effective. Sometimes you can see cloud effects in a moonlit sky. The strings of lights along the seafront of a holiday resort might make a picture. Look for floodlit buildings and fountains – the orange glow from the lights will enhance the effect in this case.

Try taking the reflections of lights on water as well: a brightly lit building with points of light reflected in a river, for example, or a lakeside restaurant with people silhouetted against the light, and splashes of light on the water.

The lights you choose must be significant enough to fill the frame. A few dots of light in the distance won't make a picture. There must be bright chunks of light near the camera, or enough light in the scene to show up the shapes of buildings or trees against the sky. After heavy rain, the streets may glisten enough to reflect back light from street lamps. Snow adds more light, so you might get a good snow scene when there are only a few actual lights in the picture.

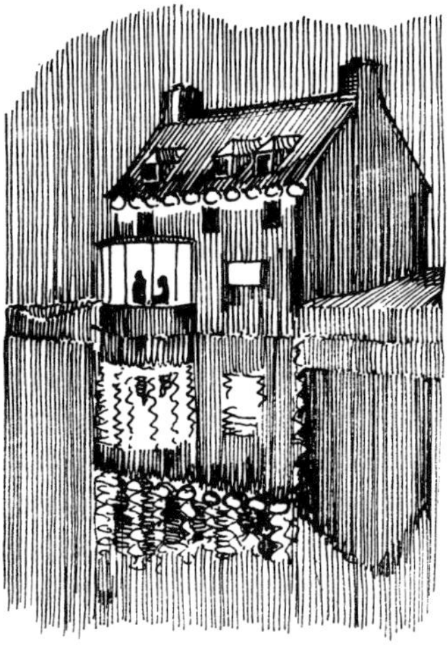

Lights reflected on water

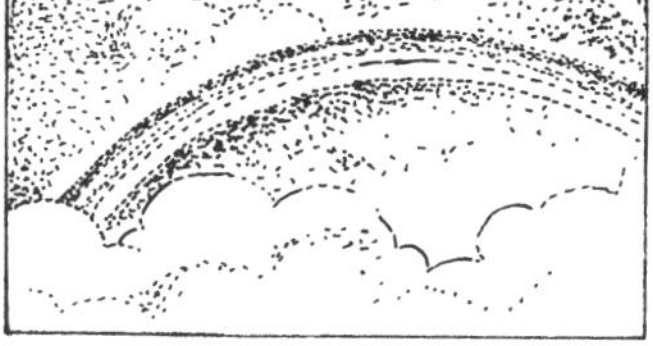

A rainbow

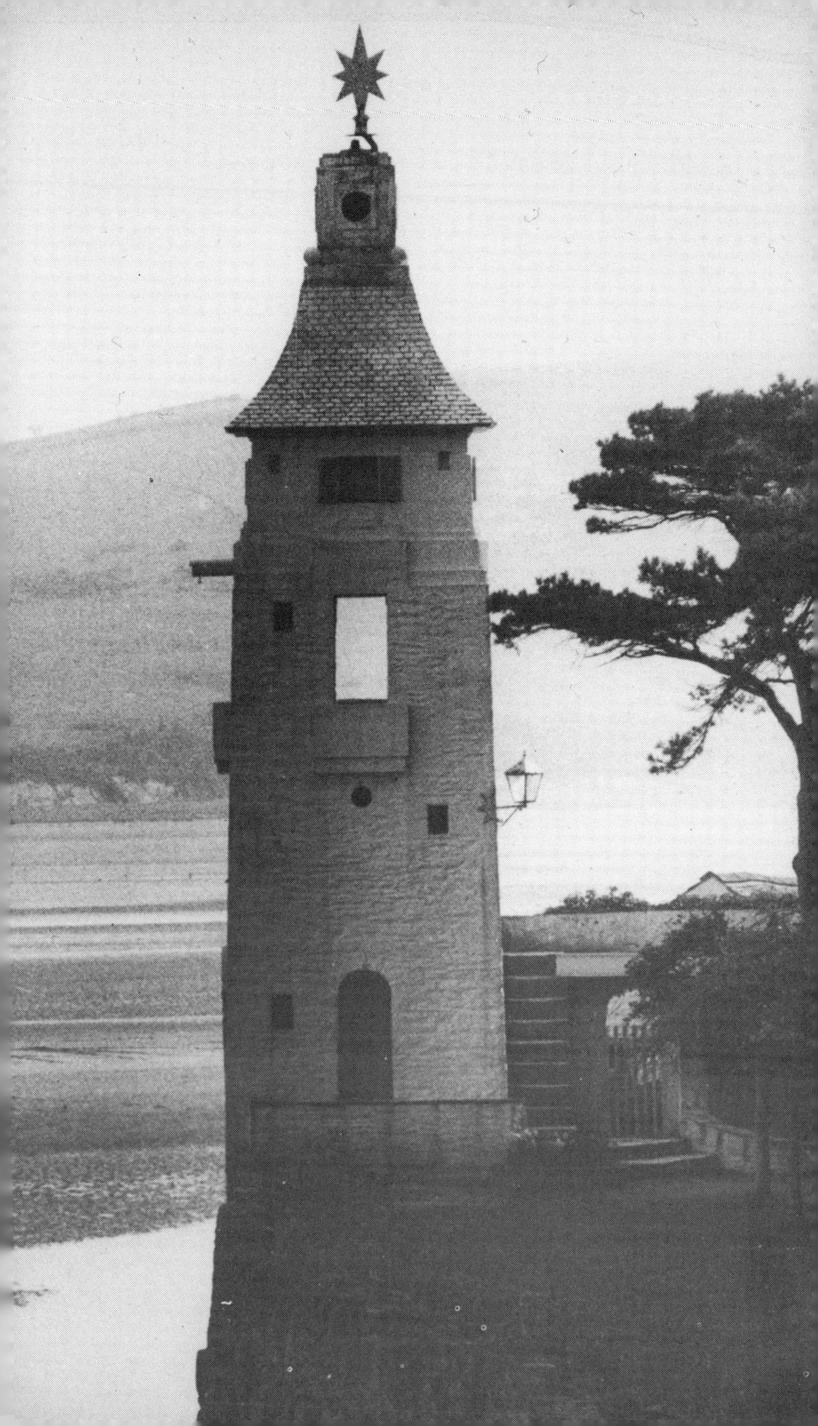

CHAPTER 9

Action Shots

If you have a camera with different shutter speeds, you can set fast speeds for action shots. This means that you can 'freeze' movement – even fast movement like motor racing or skiing.

If your camera has a fixed shutter speed, there are still ways in which you can capture movement, though you have to be more careful.

You may already have found out that if you take a picture of a moving subject with a slow shutter speed, such as 1/60, it comes out as a blur. This is because the shutter does not open and shut quickly enough to catch the subject in one place as it moves. The faster the subject is moving, the faster the shutter has to open and close to 'stop' the movement. As a general rule, choose a shutter speed of 1/500, 1/1000, or even 1/2000 if your camera allows, for fast-moving subjects, such as sport. A speed of 1/250 will stop traffic moving slowly across the frame, or people walking.

If you can't alter your shutter speed, you can't take pictures of really fast-moving subjects, but you can stop some movement by making sure moving objects are coming towards you rather than going across the frame. As a general guide, these are some shutter speeds for a car travelling at 50 kph:

Across the frame	1/500
At an angle of 45° (diagonally)	1/250
Towards or away from you	1/125

1/500

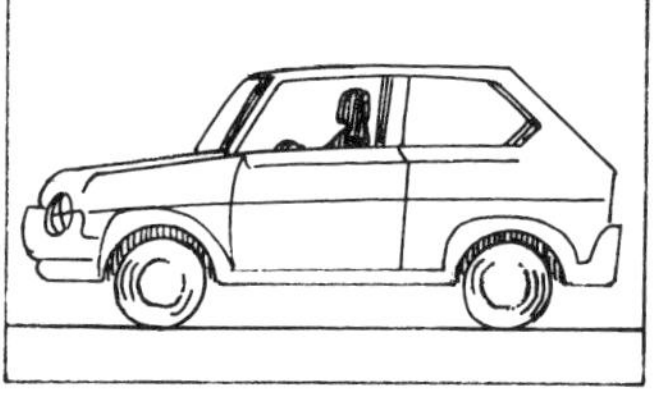

1/250

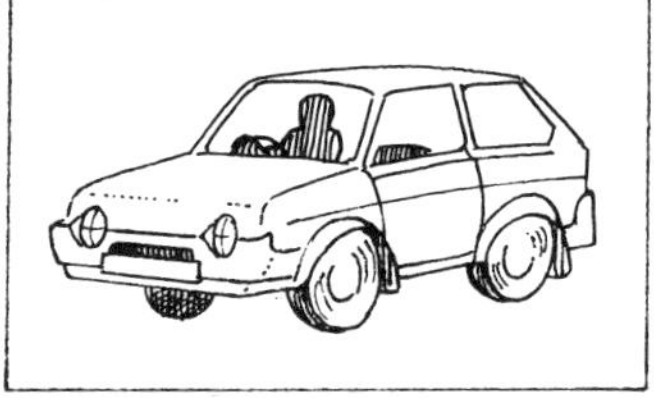

1/125

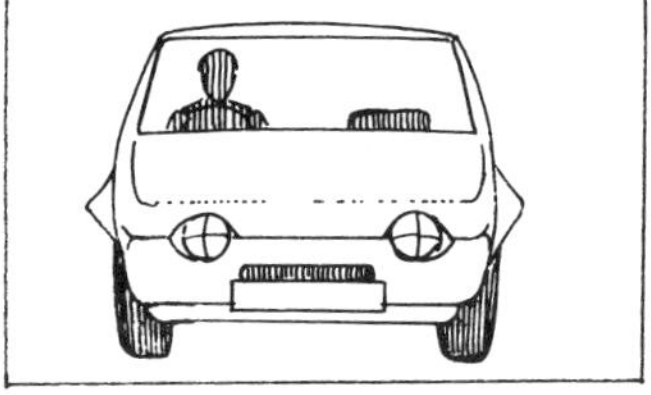

You can see that the direction makes quite a difference. Another technique is to keep moving objects at a distance. The further they are from the camera, the less blurred they will be. In the examples in the table, the car would be about 8 metres away from the camera. If it was only 4 metres away, the shutter speeds would be 1/1000, 1/500 and 1/125 in the three cases given (half the exposure time for half the distance), but if it was 16 metres away – double the distance – the speeds would be 1/250, 1/125 and 1/60, or double the exposure time.

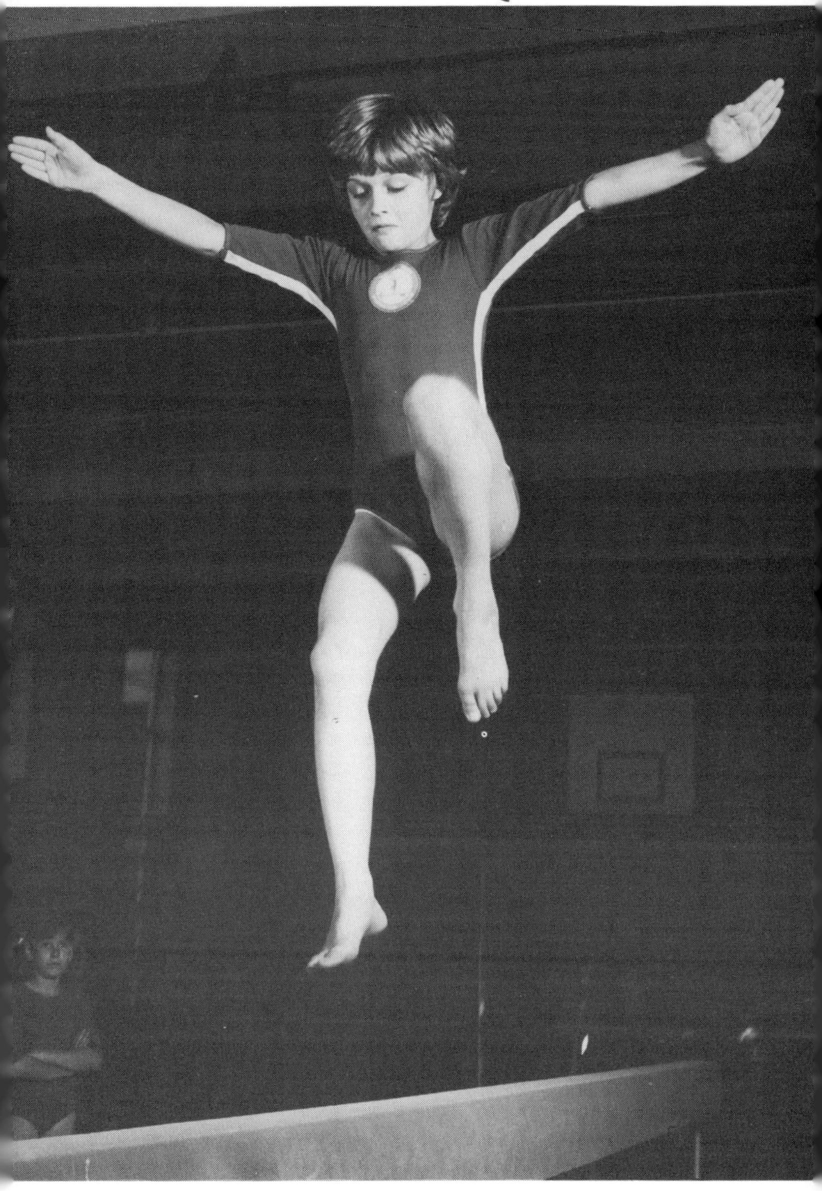

Sometimes a blurred subject against a sharp background creates a feeling of speed, but it must not be too blurred, or the picture will be spoilt.

You can keep the moving object sharp and have a blurred background. To achieve this, you use a technique called PANNING, which means following the movement with the camera. Panning is also useful if the movement is too fast to catch even with your fastest shutter speed.

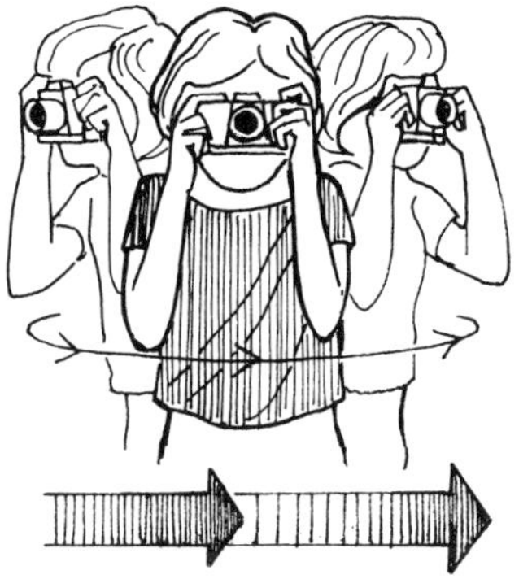

Panning the camera

Suppose you want to take a picture of a racing car. Prepare yourself before the car reaches you. Stand facing the point at which you want to take your picture. Look through the viewfinder and swing your body round to frame the approaching car. Follow it with your camera, keeping it in the centre of the frame, until it is in the position you have chosen. Press the shutter release, following the car all the time. The panning movement must be smooth from start to finish, so practise the swing before taking any pictures.

If you pan the camera, you can take moving subjects at 1/125 or even 1/60 sometimes, so you can use the technique with non-adjustable cameras as well. The background will be blurred because you have moved the camera, and this gives an effective impression of speed.

With some types of movement, there is a moment of stillness when you can take a clear picture with quite a slow shutter speed, such as 1/60. Someone on a swing, jumping in the air, swinging a golf club – all will have a moment of stillness at the end of the upward swing, just before the start of the downward swing. Wait for this precise moment and the subject will be quite still. Study the movement first so that you spot the moment of stillness, and practise catching it in the viewfinder before you take any pictures.

Find the moment of stillness

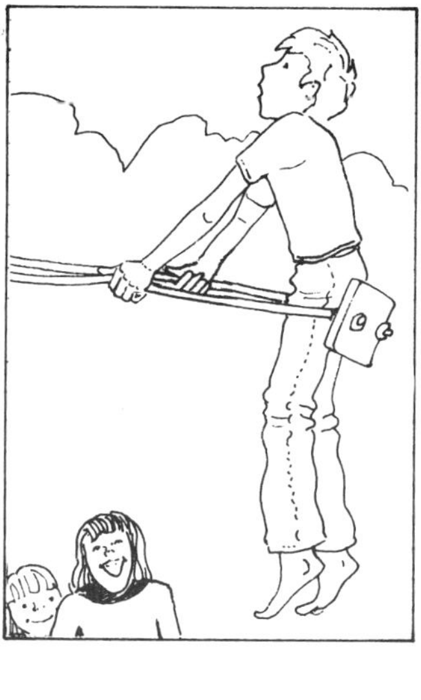

CHAPTER 10

Photographing Animals

As with all photography, taking pictures of animals needs some planning. It also takes patience and maybe some wasted film to get just the picture you want.

Pets

Dogs are probably the most easily controlled pets, in that they are used to taking orders. Try to capture the animal's character in your pictures. Perhaps have a dog sitting looking alertly at the camera, lying down with head on paws, or whatever is a characteristic pose for the animal. Maybe a study of the dog's head would look better than a full picture. The picture might be improved by including a person with the animal, showing the affection between them.

Think carefully about the background and how close you want to be to the dog. The closer the better is normally the answer, unless you want the dog to be part of a larger scene.

Take an exposure reading, bearing in mind the contrast between the dog and the background. A black dog against a light background will cause problems: either you will lose detail in the dog, which will come out as a black mass, or the background will be over-exposed. Use one of the techniques described earlier for overcoming this (bracket exposures, or choose a setting between the reading for the dog and the reading for the background). Or perhaps you can take a close-up of the dog, cutting out most of the background. Another possibility might be to put the background out of focus with a large aperture, taking an accurate exposure reading for the dog.

The way in which you choose to deal with this type of problem depends entirely on the kind of picture you want, so think carefully before deciding, and experiment with different angles and distances in the viewfinder.

For a picture of the dog posing for the camera, attract its attention when you are ready to take the picture, by calling its name or making a noise. If it isn't feeling obedient, give it a toy to play with or ask someone to keep it occupied while you take the picture.

If you want to take a picture of the dog playing and running, select a faster shutter speed (1/500) to freeze its movement. If you can't alter the speed on your camera, try panning.

Cats make good subjects, but as they are not usually interested in working to order, you may have to wait around or seek them out to catch the best pictures. Photograph your cat or kitten washing, eating, playing, sleeping, climbing, or just sitting lost in thought.

Choose the background carefully. A tabby cat, for example, will look effective against a plain carpet. Again, make sure the subject fills the frame.

When small animals are on the ground, it makes a better picture if you get down to their level. Very small animals, such as hamsters, may be a problem unless you can get very close, and for this you need a close-up lens. Unless your standard lens focuses down to less than a metre, the animal will look too small and the background too large.

If you can't get close enough to make a good picture of the animal on its own, include something else. Sit it on someone's hand or shoulder, for example, and include the person's face in the picture. You could also photograph a hamster sitting on its cage, or inside the cage. If

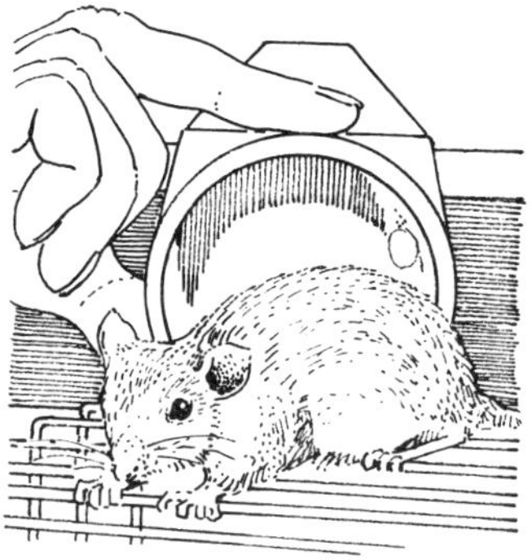

Put a small pet on its cage

your camera allows, you can put the bars of the cage out of focus. Open up to as wide an aperture as you can and put the lens of the camera right against the bars. Focus carefully on the animal and the bars in front will be lost.

Small animals in glass cages can be photographed by pressing the lens against the glass. First make sure the glass is clean and that there are no reflections.

Another way of containing small, active animals, including puppies and kittens, is to put them into something, such as a basket or a bucket, and take the

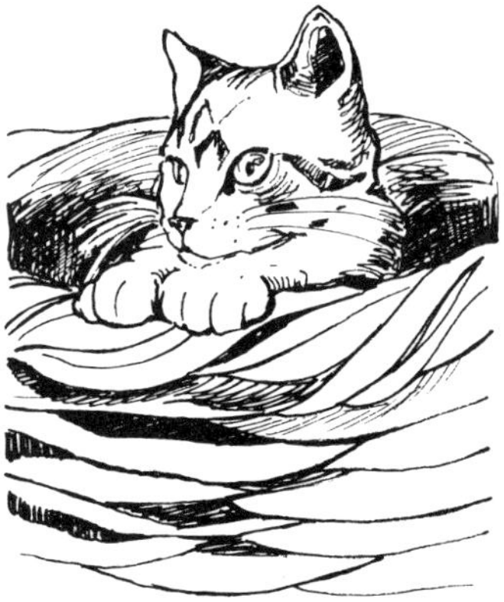

Put a kitten in a basket

picture as they are working out how to escape.

Horses are best photographed being held by the bridle. Look at the horse from different viewpoints and decide which you prefer – a side view is normally better than head-on. Arrange for the person and the horse to be looking in the same direction, and make some noise as you take the picture so that the horse's ears are up and it looks alert.

If you have a telephoto lens, you can get many more pictures of animals when they don't know you are around, or when they are in otherwise inaccessible positions. A cat climbing a tree or snoozing on a wall, or a horse grazing in a field become suitable subjects with a telephoto lens, whereas they might just be dots on the horizon with a standard lens.

If you want to photograph your pet indoors, look at the section on lighting before you begin. Animals do not like flash, and cats are afraid of it. If you do use flash, bounce it rather than shining it directly at the animal. Direct flash will frighten the animal, and the light shining in its eyes will make them look glassy.

Available light is better if there is enough of it. Choose a sunny room and encourage your pet to play or sit near the window.

Wildlife

You need even more patience to photograph wild animals and birds than you do with pets. Wild animals are normally timid and

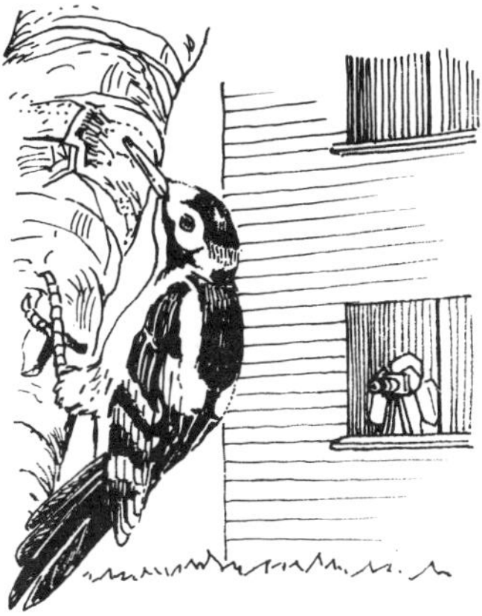

Take pictures through a window

often hide away in dark corners where they can't be seen. A telephoto lens makes life easier, but you can get pictures without one if you are prepared to wait.

If you have a garden, you could make a start there. Put out food for birds and squirrels, and then wait quietly until they are used to your presence and come to eat. You can also wait inside your house, out of sight, and take pictures through a window. A local park with water birds on the pond might be another good place to start, because the birds and animals will be used to people coming to feed them.

If you want to take wildlife pictures in the countryside, study your area first. Notice what sorts of birds and animals there are. There may be larger animals, such as deer and wild ponies, for example, or you may see a fox or a badger, as well as squirrels and rabbits. When you have chosen your area (don't forget the position of the sun), be prepared to wait for a long time.

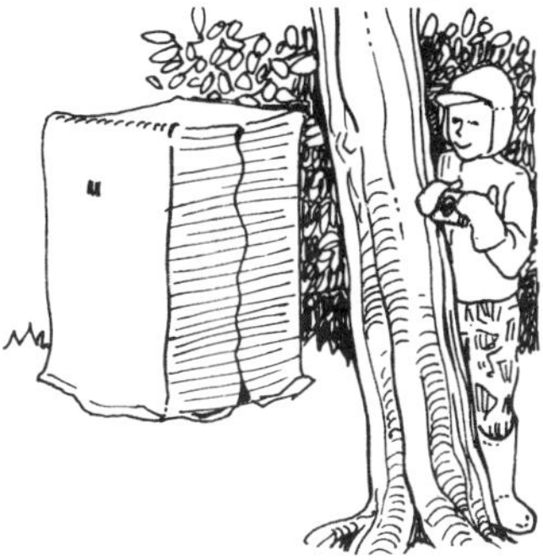

Two methods of concealment

Wear clothes that merge in with the background and wait facing the wind so that the animals won't catch your scent and be frightened off. If necessary, make a hide from branches and leaves.

Set your camera for the conditions, so that when an animal appears you just have to focus. Choose a fast shutter speed if you can, but remember that you need depth of field as well. Take several shots of an animal to give more chance of getting a good photograph.

Zoos and Safari Parks

Animals in zoos cannot run away, but they are sometimes in cages and the bars might spoil a picture. With an adjustable camera, you can put the bars out of focus by using a large aperture and standing as close to them as possible. (Never poke the lens between the bars, and don't go too close if the animal is dangerous.)

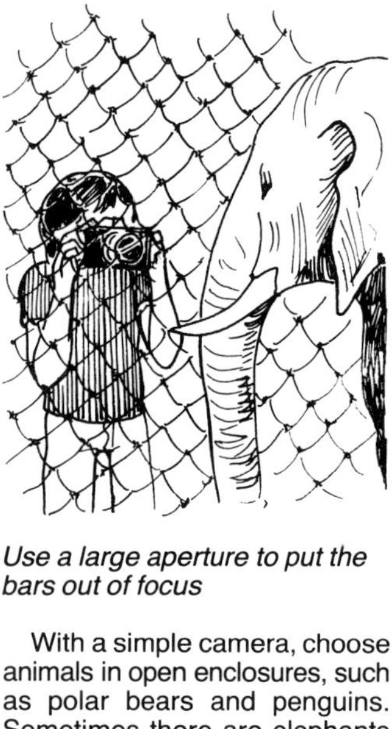

Use a large aperture to put the bars out of focus

With a simple camera, choose animals in open enclosures, such as polar bears and penguins. Sometimes there are elephants or other animals giving rides, and these make good pictures, too.

Don't be content to take pictures of an animal at the other side of its cage. It will be too small, and there will be too much uninteresting foreground in the photographs. Wait until it comes close to you, or move round the cage if you can. Remember to take light readings for the animals themselves – if they are in the shade, that is what you should expose for, even if you are in the sun.

In safari parks you must stay in the car, but it is still possible to take pictures. Make sure the car windows are clean, and never be tempted to open them. If the car has stopped, press the lens against the glass to take the picture. When the car is moving, try to hold the camera steady without touching the glass, or the vibration will cause blur.

When you are setting the controls, remember to take readings for the conditions outside the car, where the animals are. They may be some distance away, but still make interesting subjects if they are in attractive surroundings.

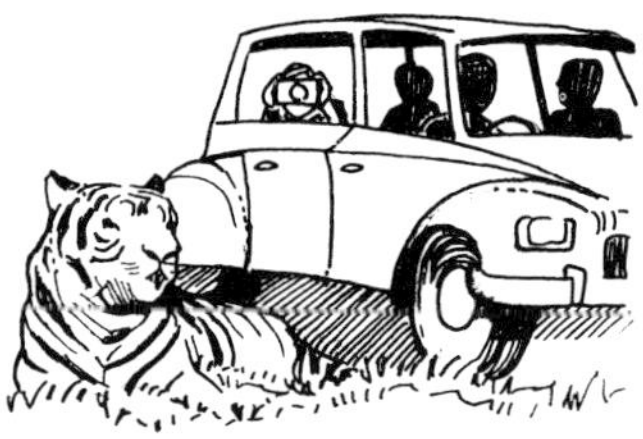

Stay in the car and take photographs through the window

Right: ask someone to attract your pet's attention so that he looks alert

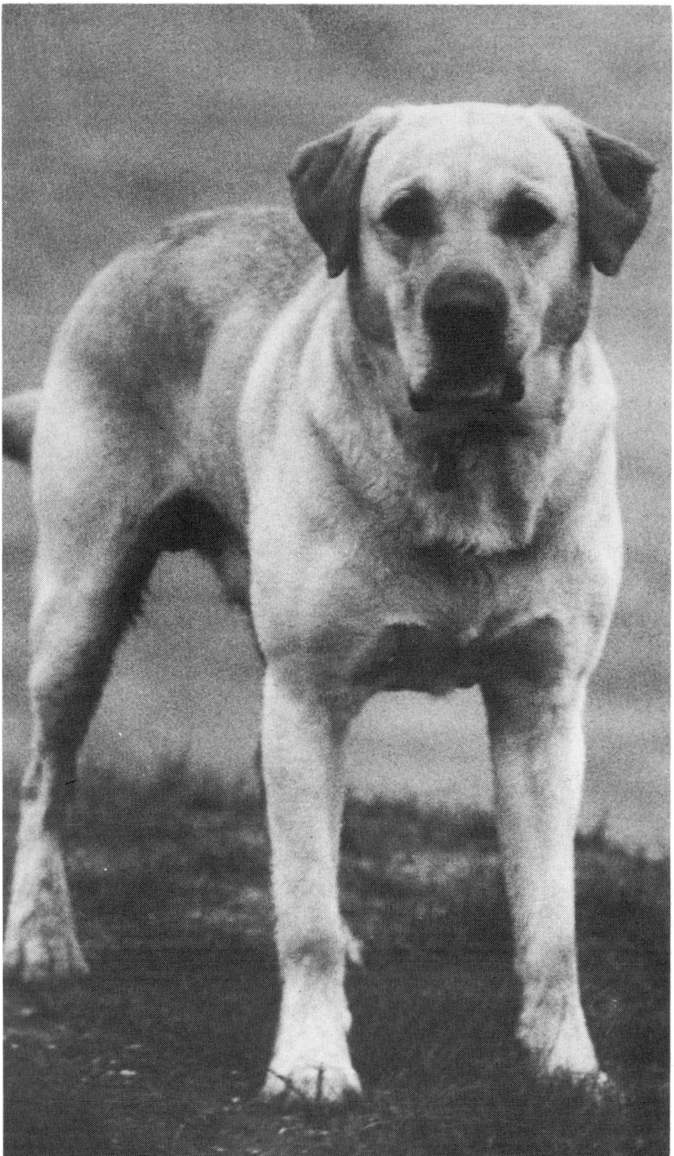

CHAPTER 11

Photographing People

Pictures of people are not as easy as they seem, because all too often the result is a stiff, unnatural pose. The aim with pictures of people is to get a relaxed expression and a natural-looking pose.

It often looks best if people are doing something, rather than staring at the camera. Even if they are not doing anything in particular, try to arrange things so that they are looking at something other than the camera (but not out of the picture). They could look at something above the camera, or over your shoulder or just to one side of you.

As with any other focal point, a person looks best positioned slightly to one side rather than in the middle of the frame. The background should be plain and preferably of a colour that makes the subject stand out. Sometimes it is effective to have the background out of focus, or partly out of focus. If you want the background to be in focus, remember to choose an aperture that gives depth of field.

Before you take the picture, decide which pose will suit your particular subject – full face or half-profile, doing something or not, and so on. Everyone is different, and a photograph should be an individual study which brings out a subject's best points. You have probably heard people say, 'I always look awful in photographs!' This could be because no one has bothered to work out how they would look best. People will always be delighted with well-thought-out pictures of themselves.

Decide on the position of the sun. Don't have it behind the subject unless you want a silhouette, and don't have it shining into his eyes as this will make him squint. Check that the sun is not casting ugly shadows on the person's face.

Make sure that the subject fills the frame and remember that even if you want to include some surroundings, the person must be recognisable as the main focal point. (You should not really be more than 3 metres away if the person is the main subject.) You may want to pose your subject sitting or leaning against a wall or a gate to give a more relaxed look. A seated person should be photographed from one side, as his knees will look enormous if they are much nearer the camera than the rest of him. Never cut a person off below the knees – this looks very odd. If people are standing, always cut above the knee – say, at thigh level – if you don't want a full-length picture.

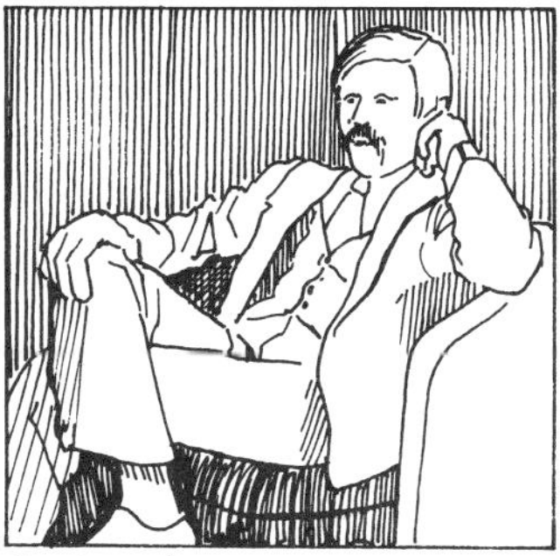

A relaxed pose

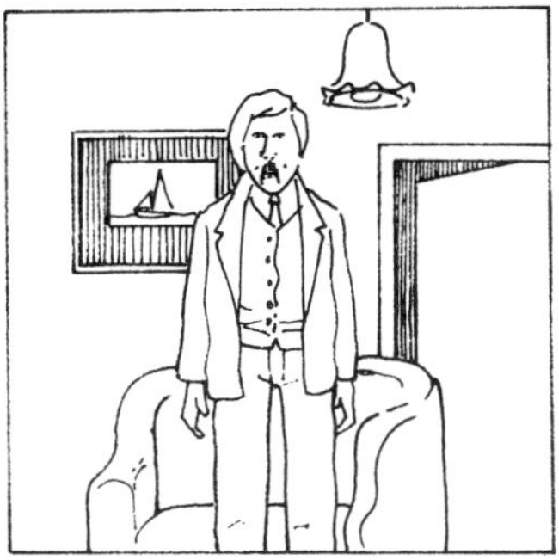

This man looks stiff and bored

Try to work most of this out before you pose the person. It is hard for someone to conjure up a natural expression if they have been hanging around waiting for the photographer to get organised. If you take too long, the person will look bored and uncomfortable instead of pleasant and relaxed. Set your camera up quickly, focus, frame the picture carefully and press the shutter release.

Groups of People

Groups of people can be formal or informal. A formal group is one in which all the people are positioned so that they can be seen (in wedding photographs, for example), but just because a group is posed in this way, it need not look stiff and awkward. Once again, positioning is very important.

Arrange the group so that everyone can be seen. Stand taller people at the back, have others sitting or perhaps perched on the arms of a chair. Some people can sit on the floor at the front. The picture will look more interesting if the people are at different levels from top to

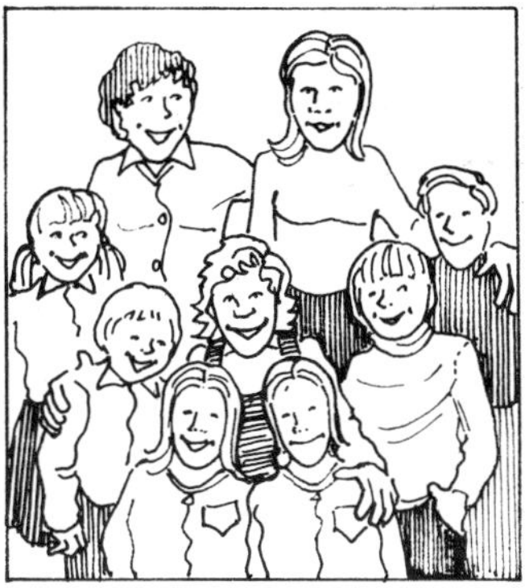

A good grouping

bottom of the frame. Arrange them in a slight semi-circle rather than straight lines.

It is very important that the group looks as if it belongs together. People should be close to each other and all looking in the same direction. They could look at the camera or at a central person in the group. Make sure that no one is looking out of the picture or in a different direction to everyone else.

Having organised the group, wait until everyone looks settled and relaxed before taking your picture. If you want to be sure of it, it is probably best to take more than one picture in case someone blinks or looks away as you press the shutter release. This sort of photograph can look very attractive if it is properly handled.

Try to catch people laughing and smiling rather than looking serious or, worse, bored. Once again, don't take too long once you have started to organise them. Set up your camera while they are still settling themselves, then all you have to do is focus and check the composition.

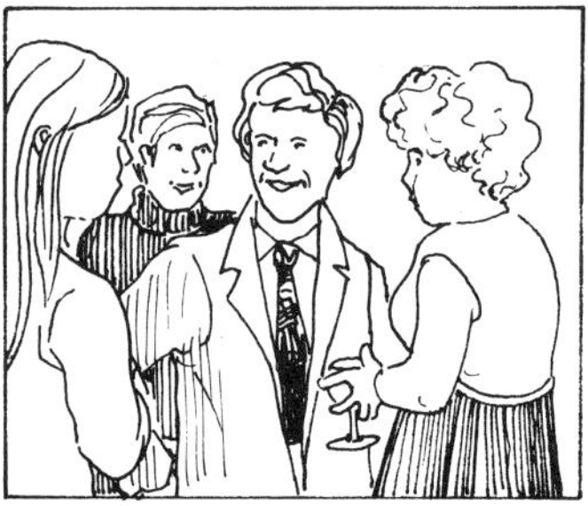

A well-positioned group

Informal groups happen rather than being arranged, but they still need care. You might want a picture of a group of people absorbed in some activity, or a crowd watching an event, such as a play or a football match. People chatting at a party or engaged in a discussion at a meeting could make an informal group. You have no power to move them around for your composition, so you must move around yourself or wait till they are well-positioned.

It is not so important that each face is seen in an informal group, but avoid a higgledy-piggledy appearance with bits of faces, arms and legs cut off. People will move more than in a formal line-up, so you have to get your camera ready, wait for your moment and then take your picture quickly. Have your camera all set up beforehand, if it is adjustable, and make sure that you have a fairly fast shutter speed and enough depth of field. Try to catch interesting expressions rather than frowns and blinks.

If there are a lot of people – in a football crowd, for example – pick out a few to concentrate on. Possibly just one face might form the true focal point. Frame the picture carefully, so that the people you have chosen fill the frame well. This will look more effective than a mass of faces.

Babies and Small Children

Try to take photographs of small children at play, when they don't realise they are being photographed. You can take spontaneous pictures and catch lively expressions, if you wait for your moment. (Posed pictures of children are not so good as they will probably look bored or self-conscious.) Choose a time when the children are against a suitable plain background, such as a carpet, the grass or the sky, or use a large aperture to put a distracting background out of focus – but remember that you must focus very carefully. Set your camera for the conditions, choosing a shutter speed of at least 1/250 so that you can freeze a child's movement if you need to.

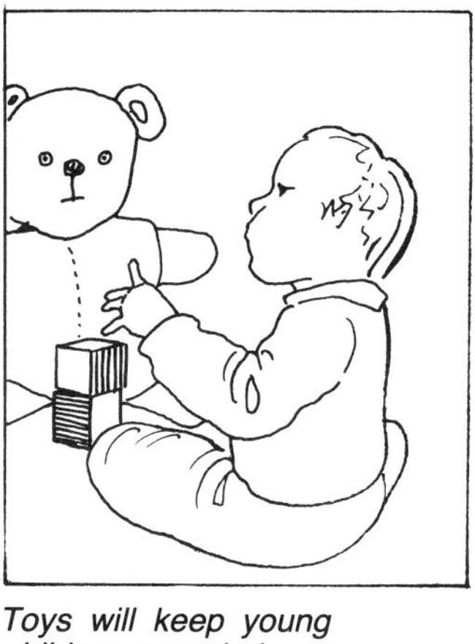

Toys will keep young children occupied

If a child knows you are there and seems self-conscious, wait until he has forgotten about you and is absorbed in a game. A telephoto lens is useful, because you can keep your distance, yet still focus on lively expressions and concentrate on the children playing. Get down to their level and make sure you really fill the frame.

With a non-adjustable camera, choose a moment when a child is playing in good light and is absorbed in a fairly static game, so that the pictures aren't spoilt by the blur of movement.

Available light pictures of children playing indoors can be effective. Avoid a posed look by arranging for the children to play by a window, and then wait until they have forgotten you. If you want to take flash pictures, bounce the flash rather than using it direct.

Tiny babies don't move around so much, but they can be difficult because they are so small. If you are photographing the baby on its own, get as close as you can, so that the baby fills the frame, and put any fussy background out of focus. Sometimes it is best to take a small baby with his mother. For one thing, you don't have to get so close to fill the frame, and for another you can take enchanting pictures showing the bond between mother and baby. Wait till they are playing, or the mother is bathing the baby, and take non-posed, natural pictures.

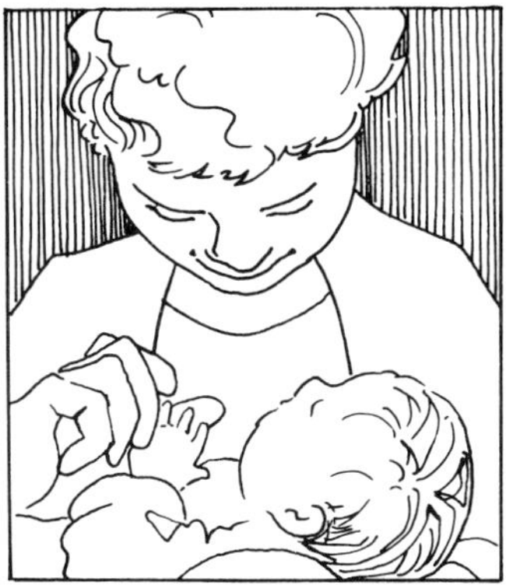

Pose the baby with its mother

If there is a young baby or toddler in your own family, you can keep a delightful photographic record as the child grows up. If you want to photograph a friend's baby, make sure the family are all happy to have you around. They will probably be delighted to have good pictures of their child.

Candid Pictures

The term 'candid' is used to describe pictures of people who don't know they are being photographed. Of course, if there is any chance that they will notice you, you must make sure that they don't mind. For example, people at work or absorbed in some task may realise that they are being photographed, but if they don't mind and just carry on with what they are doing, you will get what looks like a candid shot.

A telephoto lens is very useful, because you can stand some distance away, merging with the background, and close in on people's faces.

Without a telephoto lens, you will need to be more discreet, as you will have to be fairly close to the subject. The minute you raise your camera to your eye, you attract attention and the picture may be spoilt.

Set the controls on your camera in advance, choosing a fairly fast shutter speed and a small enough aperture to give you good depth of field. (Make sure that the film you are using is fast enough to cope with this combination.) Focus on something which you judge to be the same distance away as your subject. (Good depth of field will allow for mistakes here.) Only then should you turn to your subject. Raise your camera to your eye and take the picture quickly. Another way is to pretend you are taking a picture of something else, then at the last minute swing round to frame your chosen subject.

For this sort of approach you need to practise judging distances, so you don't waste time moving or re-focusing before taking the picture.

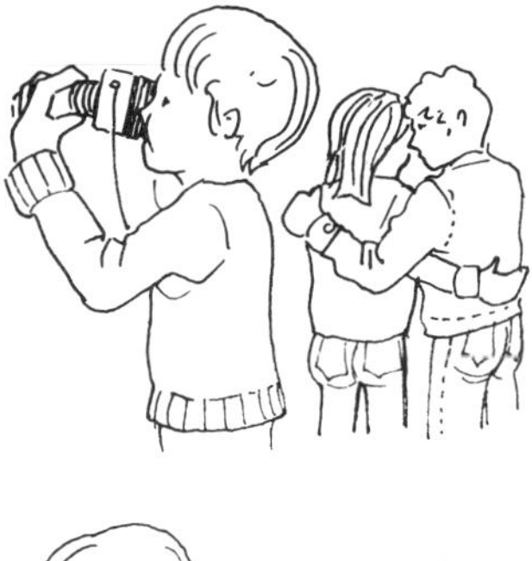

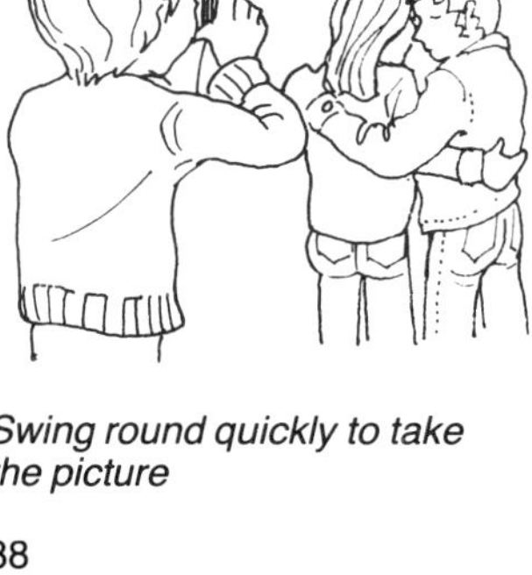

Swing round quickly to take the picture

If your camera is non-adjustable, you don't have to worry about the controls, but you must make sure that the conditions are right. You need good light and a fairly static subject.

Candid pictures crop up all over the place. Sometimes faces in a crowd are good, and the more absorbed people are, the less likely they are to notice you. Wander round with your camera, framing different subjects, so that people get used to your presence. Look for expressions, and pictures which tell a story. A photograph won't be interesting unless there is something about the subject that appeals.

Indoors, try to take candid pictures by available light rather than flash – flash will attract the subject's attention. Take light readings from areas with the same or similar light. If you take the reading with a hand-held meter, this will be less noticeable than a through-the-lens system.

Portraits

A portrait is a study of a person's face and this is what you should concentrate on when composing one. Lighting is very important, and so is the angle of the head and the view of the face. As with all pictures of people, you want to catch your subject's best points and take a photograph which shows his character. Although the picture is posed, you want it to look 'real'.

It is normally best to take several pictures for the same portrait and then decide which you like most. Experiment with different lighting and positions for each shot. Sometimes just a tiny movement to one side can alter the whole look of the picture. A subject posing for a portrait won't mind you taking your time if the result is a really good picture that is just like him.

You can take portraits indoors under studio conditions – that is, with extra lighting (see page 59) but you can just as easily take them out of doors in sunlight, or indoors using available light. The main thing is for the light to be shining on the face so that there aren't any unpleasant shadows, yet the features and the shape of the face are picked out.

Backgrounds for portraits should be completely plain. Put the background out of focus if you are outside and there are trees and greenery in the way. Focusing should not be a problem with a subject who is posing for you. You should compose the picture in a vertical frame and get close enough for the head and shoulders to fill the picture. Sometimes a telephoto lens is useful for portraits as you can fill the frame with head and shoulders without being too close to the subject.

Ask your subject to move his head to different positions and decide whether to take a profile (side view) or half-profile, whether he should look at the camera or slightly to one side, whether he should look up or look down, smile or look serious. Take pictures of different positions, but before you do, check the whole picture, not just the face. Make sure that the altered angles don't cause ugly

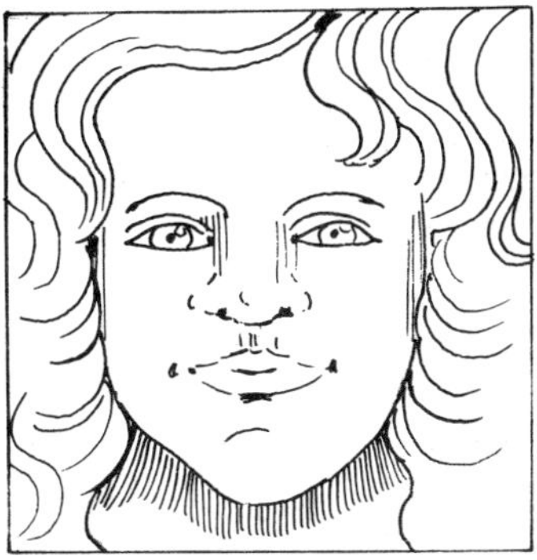

Front view

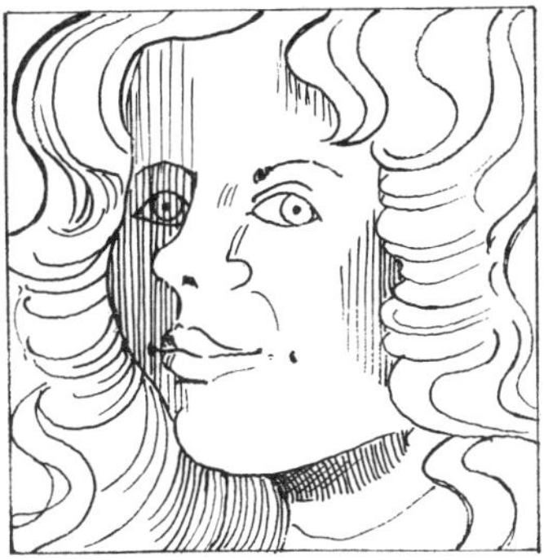

Half-profile

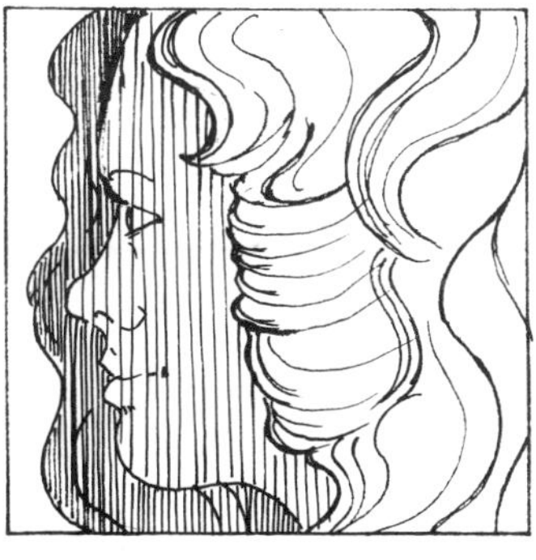

Profile

folds in the neck and that the nose isn't casting shadows on the rest of the face.

It is important to wait for a pleasant and relaxed expression for a portrait, too. As the subject becomes more used to your taking pictures, he will become more relaxed and so look less self-conscious and awkward. Tell him when you are taking a picture, so that he doesn't blink or move at the crucial moment.

The lighting directions are of course the same as for other types of photograph, but you need to think of the effect this will have on a face. Front lighting, as we have seen, casts a flat even light which may make the face look featureless and disc-like. The subject will squint if the light is bright, as it will be shining into his eyes. Back lighting produces a silhouette. Side lighting of some sort is best for most portraits, but make sure that it doesn't leave one half of the face in shadow. Try to bring out the shape of the face without too much texture (which would show up every blemish). You will probably find that half-side lighting is the most suitable, but it all depends on the individual, the setting and the lighting you are using, so do experiment.

Indoor Portraits

The last section dealt with taking portraits when there is enough natural light to hold the camera yourself. With artificial lighting, you need a tripod, as even bright lights will not give you a fast enough shutter speed to avoid camera shake and a blue filter should be used with colour film to correct that orange tinge that artificial light will give the film. If you hope to enlarge the portraits, the film should not be too fast, which would make the enlargements grainy: 125 ASA for black and white, and 100 or 200 ASA for colour would probably be the most suitable speeds. If you are not planning to make enlargements, use a faster film, such as 400 ASA, or even 1000 ASA, to give you more scope.

Professional photographic studios have all kinds of photoflood lighting to use for this sort of work, but you can achieve a good effect with bright anglepoise lights and reflectors. The idea is to get good even lighting, without heavy shadow, yet with enough light and shade to give the face character and shape. (The overhead electric light on its own will give a flat overall lighting.)

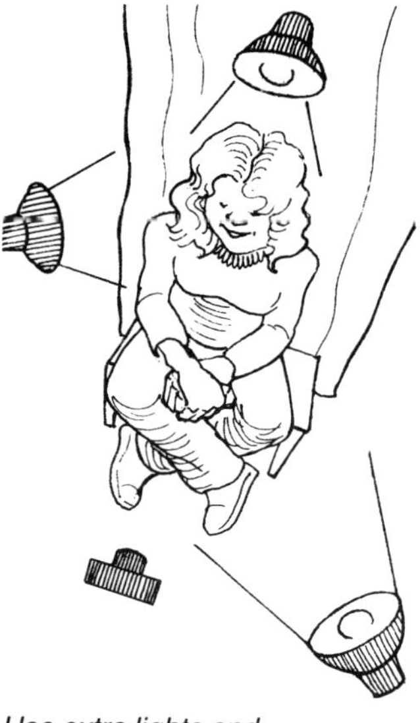

Use extra lights and a reflector

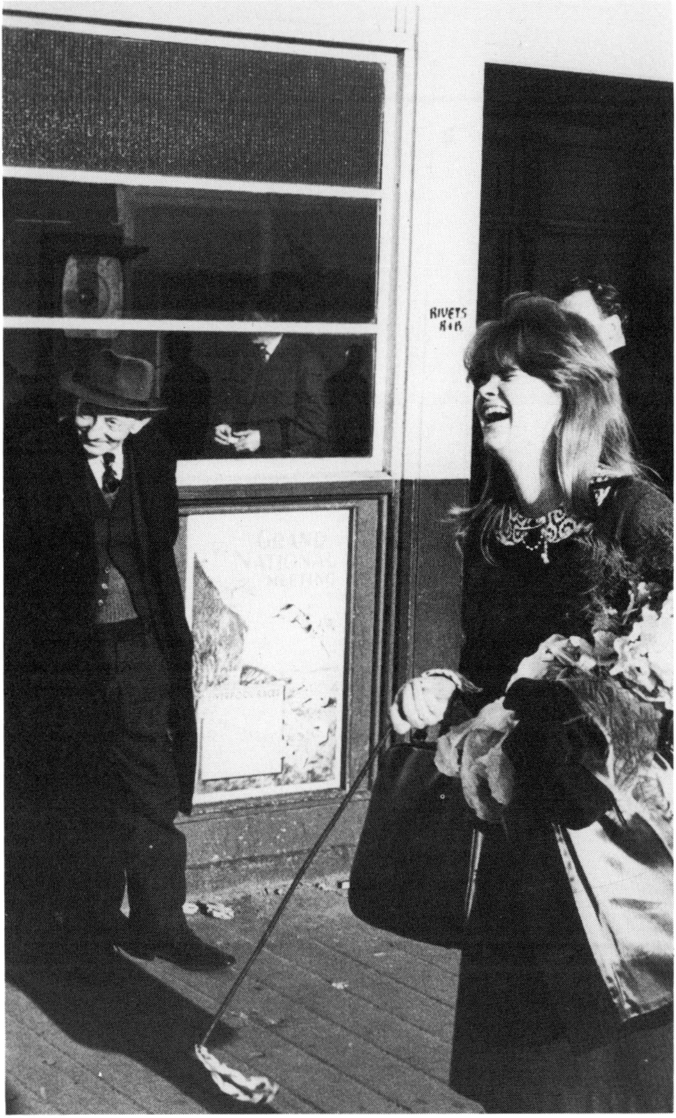

The photographer has captured the passers-by in a relaxed and happy mood

Experiment with one or two lights and a reflector made from white cloth to soften any shadows. Have one light fairly close to the model and move it round to see the effect this creates. Use a reflector or white card to brighten up shadows, and try a second light behind the model's head to lighten up the hair. Move your lights round until you are completely satisfied, noting what happens to highlights and shadows each time. Don't use too many lights as you will get a muddle of shadow and highlight which will spoil the effect.

If you want to use flash rather than artifical light, you can hold the camera yourself, and you won't have problems with colour film, but you can't create such interesting effects. Bounce the flash and, if you can, detach the flash from the camera. Use a reflector to soften any shadows.

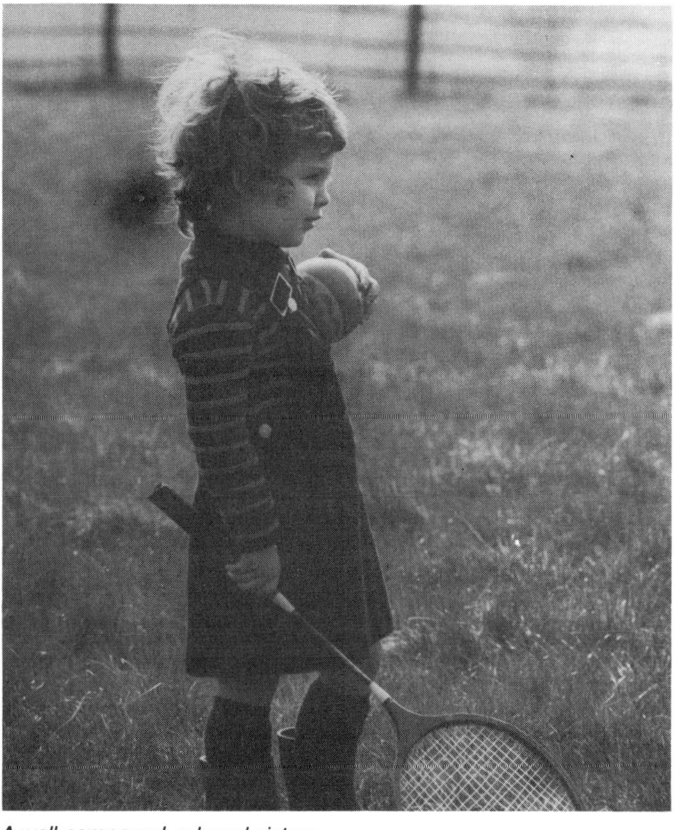

A well-composed, relaxed picture

CHAPTER 12

Still-life and Close-up Work

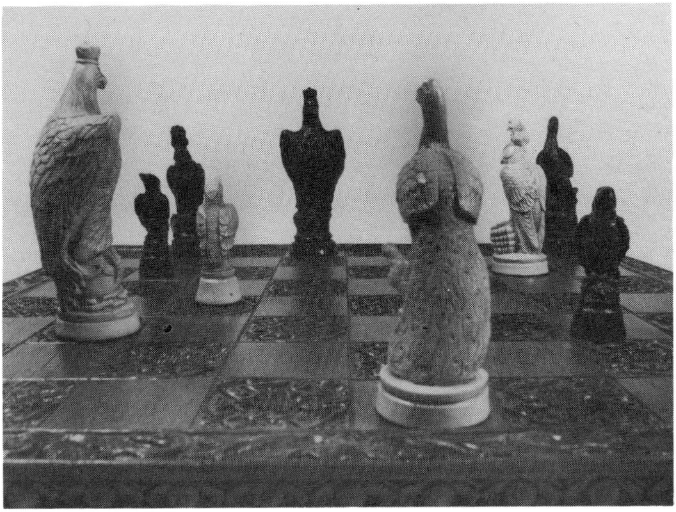

Still-life

You can take a still-life by available light, artificial light, flash or out of doors in sunlight. The beauty of this sort of picture is that there is all the time in the world to get it right as nothing will move away!

The still-life collection you are photographing must be interesting, with varying shapes and textures, and good colour combinations if you are using colour film. The lighting shouldn't be too flat, as you want highlights and shadows to bring out shape and texture. The background should be plain, or put out of focus, so that it doesn't distract. You could use a table near a window, or a windowsill with the window put out of focus, perhaps. The floor, a plain carpet, grass or plain stone-work are all suitable backgrounds, or you can make a background with a sheet of white paper pinned up behind the arrangement and curving underneath it. (Don't fold the paper as this will cause shadows on the background.)

Arrange the objects you have chosen carefully, so that the display is pleasing to the eye, and everything can be seen. A still-life must completely fill the frame, so don't choose anything small if you can't go close. An assortment of things of different sizes would probably look best. If

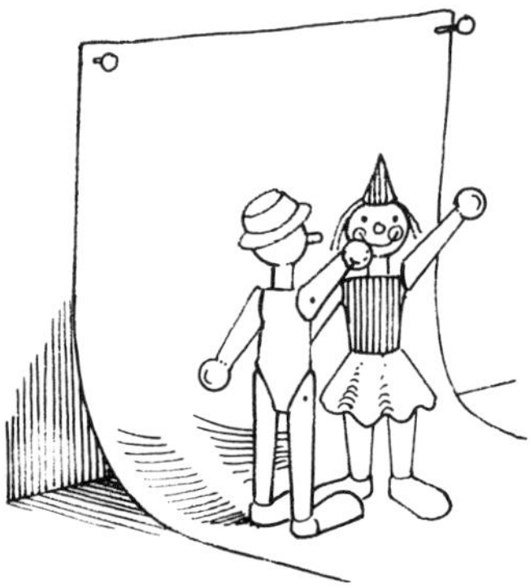

Use a sheet of white paper for a background

the objects are all low ones, crouch down to their level, or look down on them from above.

Close-up Work

You can try some sort of close-up work whatever sort of camera you have, though it is easier if you have an adjustable camera, and preferably an SLR which will accept different lenses and extension rings or tubes (see page 32). With an adjustable camera you can go up close and focus carefully for a pin-sharp image, and if you have close-up accessories, you can take pictures of tiny flowers and insects which could not be tackled with a standard lens.

With a simple camera, you are restricted by the focusing distance. Experiment to find the focusing distance of your camera. You may find that you can't go closer to your subject than 1 metre, which limits your choice of subject – but you can still try taking pictures of large flowers and shrubs, so long as they fill the frame.

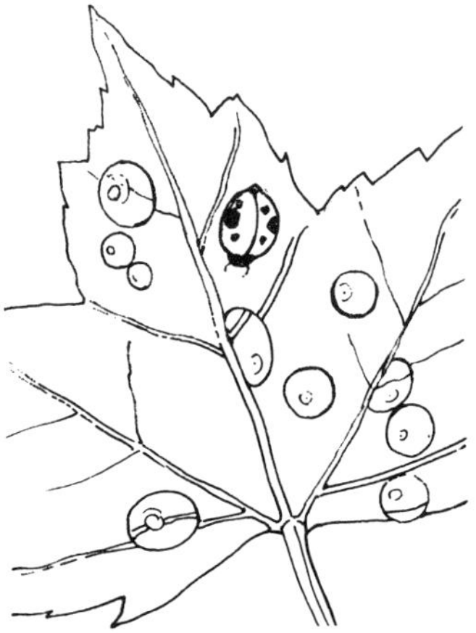

Use a leaf as background when photographing insects

If you have a standard lens, experiment carefully to find out how close you can go, and bear this in mind when you are choosing a subject. Many flowers can be photographed well with a standard lens, and so can insects such as butterflies, though they will probably need flowers or the branch of a shrub to help to fill the frame.

The background is very important in close-up work. You are aiming to bring out the detail on the petals of a flower or the wings of an insect, and so you don't want a lot of distracting foliage all around. It is normally best to put the background completely out of focus, so that the subject stands out. If you use the widest aperture your camera has – say f/2.8 or f/1.7 – there will be almost no depth of field, so you will have problems with flowers like daffodils and lilies which have long trumpets. One part of a single flower may be in focus and another part blurred. Flat shapes and flowers are best for a very wide aperture.

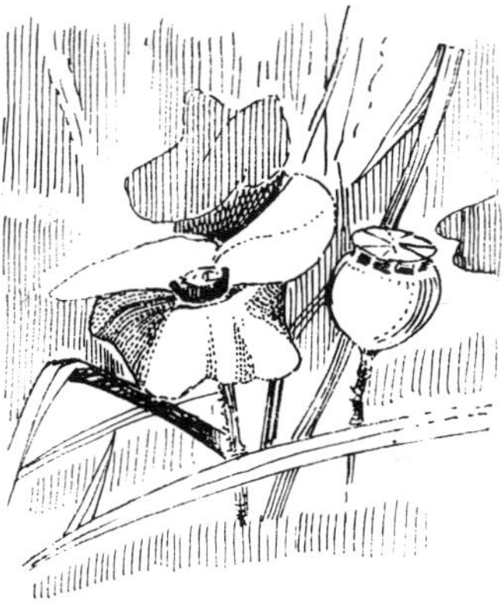

Focus on a single flower

Another reason for using a large aperture is to let plenty of light into the camera. When you are focusing close to a growing flower, very little light from the sky will be let into the lens. This particularly applies to plants in corners of woods where there is not much sunlight. Take careful readings from the subject you are photographing and decide how to balance background, depth of field and light to make the picture you want.

If you are taking photographs against the sky – a spray of flowers or an insect on a flower, say – you may have problems with too much light for your camera to cope with, particularly with a large aperture, but if the background is just sky, you don't need to put it out of focus so the aperture can be smaller. Go up close to the subject and take a reading, then make sure you fill the frame, cutting out as much sky as possible.

If it is windy, you will need a fast shutter speed to stop any movement of the plant. With a large aperture you might focus carefully on a flower, say, only to find that the wind blows it out of the depth of field at the crucial moment. So try not to choose your largest aperture under these conditions – or find flowers that are in sheltered places, out of the wind.

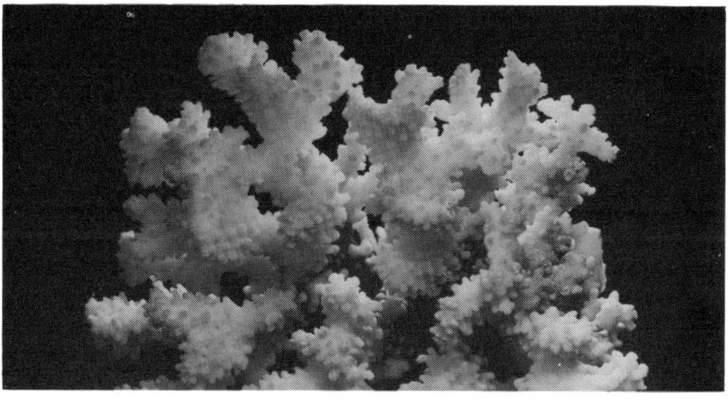

A coral makes an unusual subject

We have been dealing with all the aspects of planning and taking good photographs.

The next chapters cover the methods of developing and printing, and how to achieve special effects.

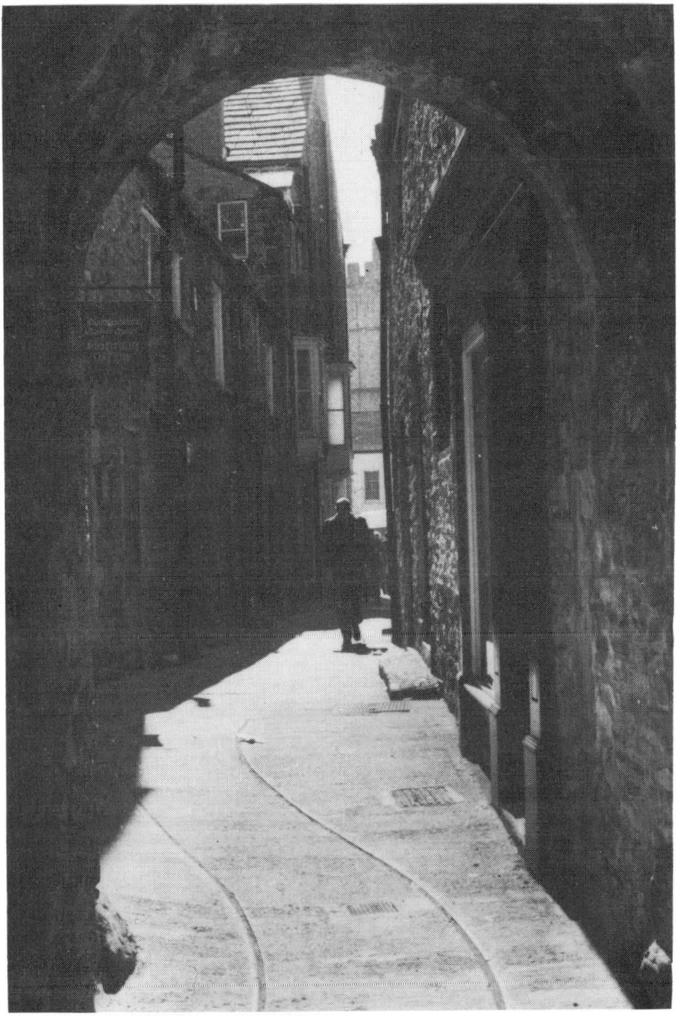

Looking for pictures can make you more aware of familiar surroundings

CHAPTER 13

Setting up a Darkroom

You will need a darkroom if you want to develop your own film and prints. An ideal solution is a big walk-in cupboard, which is already fairly dark because it hasn't any windows, but you can just as easily improvise by setting up a temporary darkroom in the bathroom. Another answer might be to make a small dark-room by dividing off part of your bedroom or another room in the house with space to spare.

What do you need for a dark-room? It is useful to have running water in the room, which is why the bathroom is a popular choice, as there are not normally any power points or light switches to worry about. (**Remember that you must never touch electrical points or switches when your hands are wet or when there is water on the floor.**) The main thing is that the room must be really dark – even a chink of light will spoil an undeveloped film – and you need a space at least 2

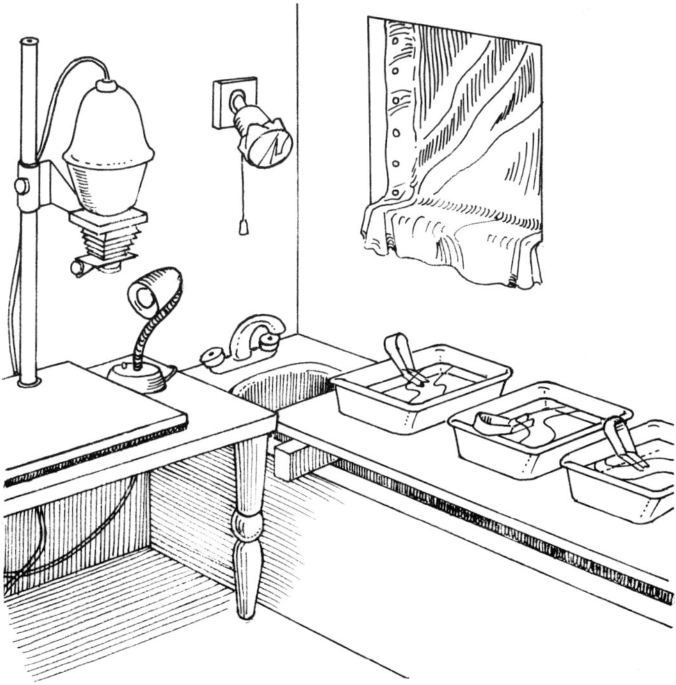

You can easily adapt your bathroom into a darkroom

metres long by about 1.5 metres wide so that you can work comfortably.

If you are using a room as a temporary darkroom, get hold of some blacking-out materials that are the right size and can be put up quickly and easily. For the windows you can use heavy dark material, such as blankets, or black plastic rubbish bags pinned tightly all the way round. If the windows aren't too big, you could make black-outs from sheets of hardboard to fit snugly against the window. The black-out must cover the whole frame, not just the glass, so that light doesn't creep round the edges.

Don't forget the keyhole, and gaps round the door. Newspaper may do for both, or a draught excluder could be used for wider gaps under the door. Masking tape is also useful for keyholes and small gaps. (You may find it easier to hang a heavy blanket over the door each time.) When you have blacked out the room, let your eyes get used to the darkness, and then check whether you have left any gaps.

If your darkroom is permanent, you can make a really thorough job of blacking everything out. Make sure that there is a lock on the door, so that people don't come in accidentally while you are working.

You need working surfaces, and cupboards or shelves to keep things in, and you need to split the room into 'wet' and 'dry' areas. The dry area is for the

A room set up permanently as a dark room

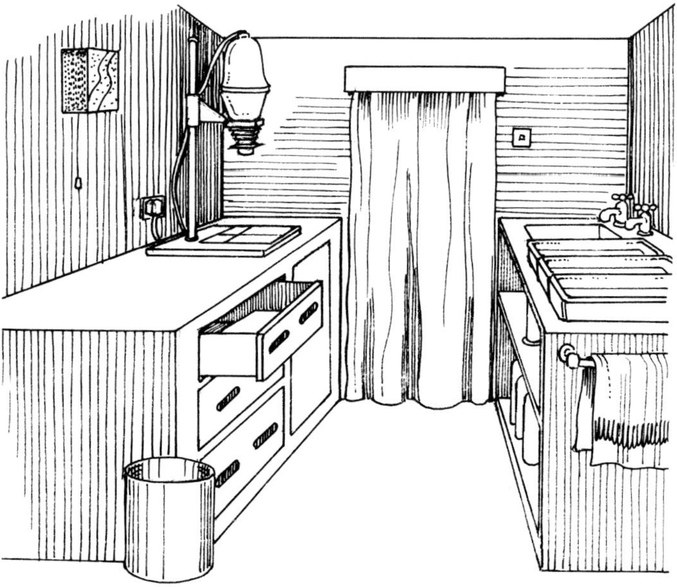

Diagram of an enlarger

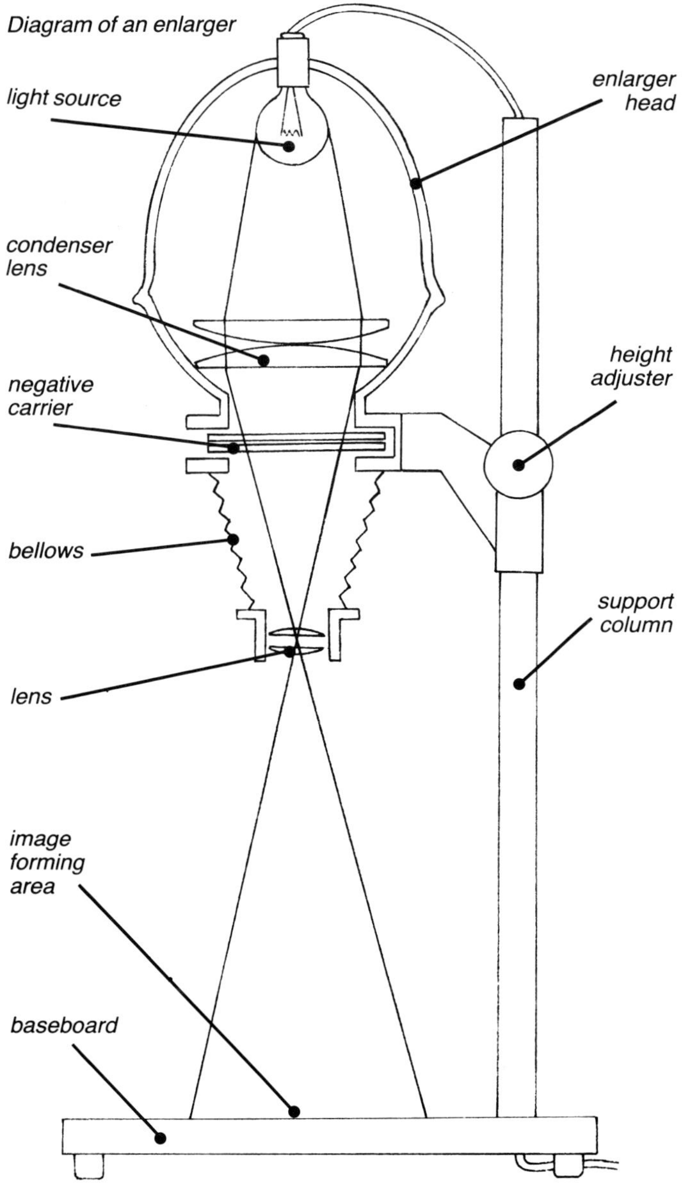

enlarger, which needs to be plugged in – if you are using a bathroom or a cupboard without a socket, you will need an extension lead. The wet area is for the trays of chemicals and the washing stages. It is important to keep them separate for your own safety. Have a towel in the darkroom, so that you can dry your hands when you have been working with liquids.

You do need light in your darkroom for the stages when it will not damage the film or photographic paper. A lamp in your dry area is the easiest, and the most effective for studying prints. You also need a red SAFELIGHT for when you are working in the dark. This is the one sort of light that won't damage your prints (though you still need to develop your film in complete darkness). You can buy safelights from photographic suppliers.

Most of the equipment you buy for your darkroom will last for many years, so although it may seem expensive, it is worthwhile if you are keen on this aspect of photography. The most expensive item will be the ENLARGER. As the name suggests, this enlarges the negative, or part of the negative, to the size of print you want.

You can often find second-hand enlargers that are in good condition. Decide whether you will be working in black and white only, or whether you might move on to colour processing later. A lot of enlargers can cope with both. Look through photographic magazines or the local paper, or have a word with a photographic dealer about the different sorts of enlarger available. You will not need a very sophisticated enlarger to start with, and you can always sell your enlarger and buy another when you are more experienced.

With your enlarger, you need a MASKING FRAME to hold the paper while printing the negative on to it, and a sheet of glass (about 20 cm by 25 cm) for making contact prints (see page 110). You can buy masking frames, or you can make one from a piece of board. You can also make a baseboard for your enlarger out of chipboard or wood. Instead of a masking frame, you could cut rectangles of wood out of the baseboard to the size of the printing papers you are using. A FOCUS FINDER is useful, but not essential. This magnifies part of the image, so you can see if your negative is correctly focused under the enlarger. A focus finder does help you to avoid fuzzy prints – sharpness is not always easy to see with the naked eye.

Top: positive image with black and white correct

Right: negative image with black and white reversed

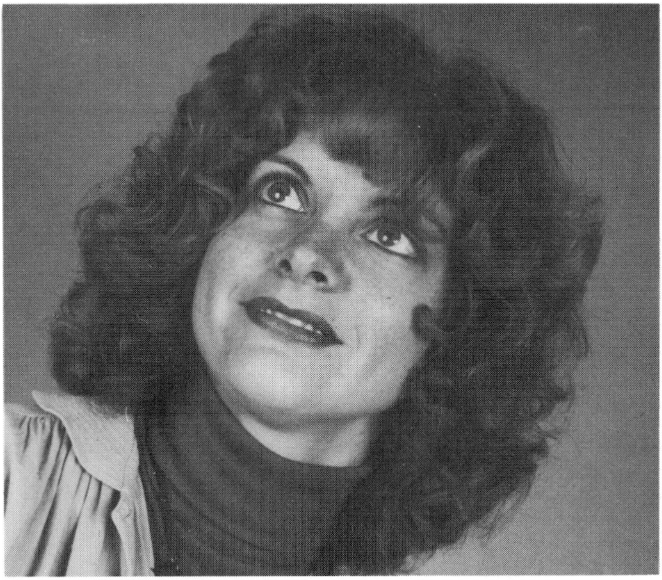

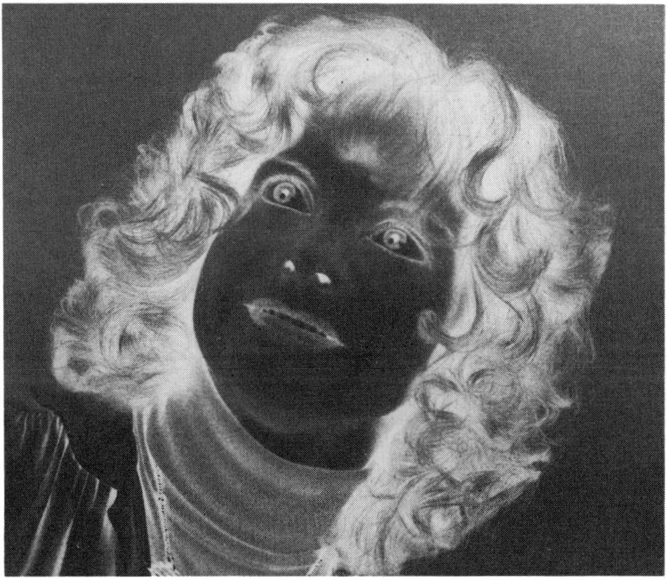

CHAPTER 14

Developing Black and White Film

Photography, particularly in black and white, becomes even more interesting if you develop and print your own pictures. Colour developing and printing is an expensive and tricky process and it is probably cheaper to use the commercial laboratories for colour prints, but developing and printing black and white pictures is not difficult and, once you have set up your darkroom, need not be too expensive. You can get just the picture you want by enlarging certain parts of a negative, lightening or darkening tones, putting right exposure errors made during picture-taking, and trying some of the special effects that are possible.

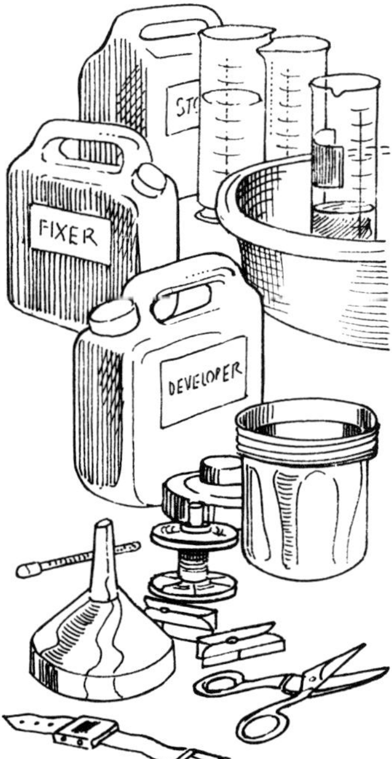

DEVELOPING the film means producing a set of negatives from which prints can be made. To do this, you need some equipment and chemicals: a DEVELOPING TANK, with spiral for winding the film on, a funnel for pouring chemicals, a clock or watch with a second hand, or a photographic stop-clock, a thermometer, developing chemicals (DEVELOPER, STOP BATH and FIXER), 3 dark bottles for storing the mixed chemicals (labelled *developer, stop* and *fixer*), 3 graduated measures (also labelled *developer, stop* and *fixer*), film clips or clothes pegs, scissors, and a washing-up bowl or plastic bucket (for waste chemicals).

You can buy all the equipment you need from a photographic shop, although some of the things on the list can be improvised from household items.

When you buy chemicals, make sure that they can be used for both developing and printing, and that they are suitable for the film you are using. Buy them in liquid rather than powder form. The liquids have to be diluted with water, but if you mix up more than you need, you can store made-up solutions in your dark airtight bottles. (These must be dark so that light doesn't get in.) You can use stop bath (which stops the developer) and fixer (which fixes the image) more than once, so pour each back

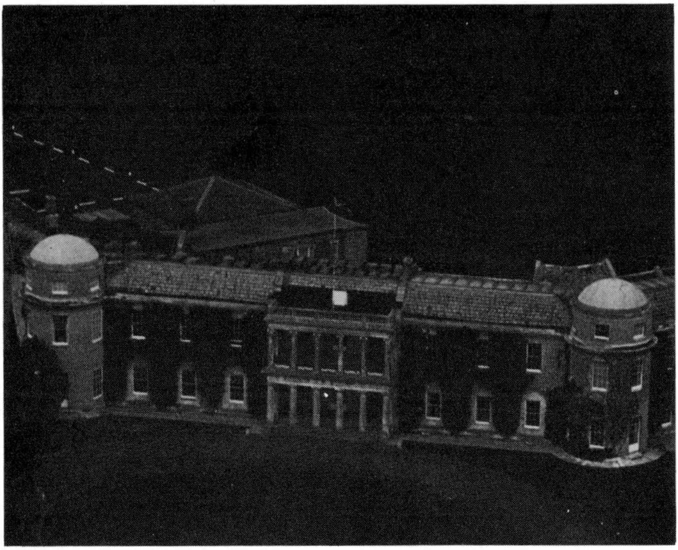
Under-exposed

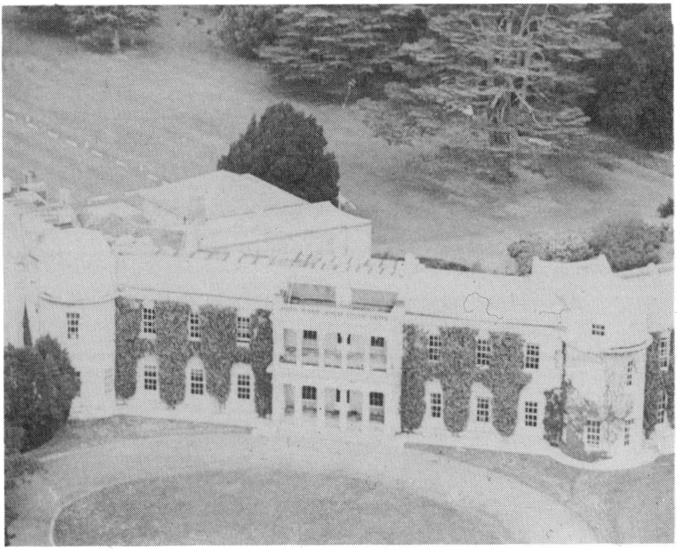
Over-exposed

into its container when you have finished with it. Developer brings out the image on the film, and loses its strength once you have used it, so it is best to throw this away each time.

This is all you need to develop a film, though you will need other equipment for printing (see pages 109–116).

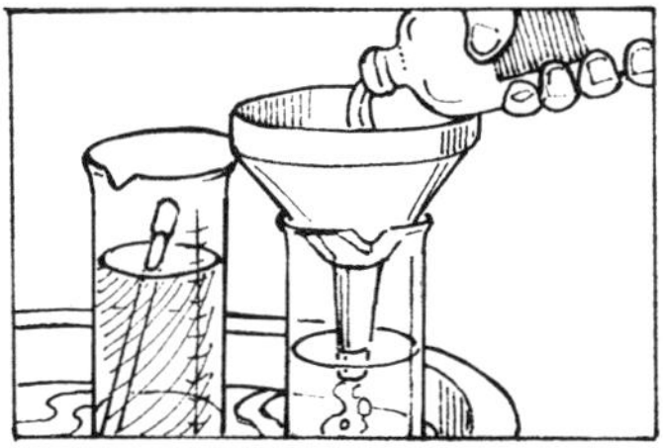

Mix the chemicals to the correct strength

Step by Step through Developing

1 Mix up your chemicals to the correct strength in the three measures. The temperature the chemicals need to be at (20°C) is important so test the water with your thermometer before diluting the chemicals. You can stand the measures in a bowl of warm water to keep the temperature even.

The amount of a chemical that you need to cover a film in your developing tank will be written on the tank, probably in fluid ounces and millilitres. The dilution instructions on the chemicals will be shown as, for example, 1 + 10. This means 1 part of chemical to 10 parts of water, so 1 fluid ounce of chemical would make 11 fluid ounces of diluted chemical.

2 Make sure that you have everything ready and within easy reach before you go any further, as the next part of the process has to be carried out in the dark.

3 You are going to load the film into the developing tank, in the dark (or you can use a CHANGING BAG for this, if you have one). Loading the film is a bit tricky until you get used to it so it is worth practising on a bit of waste film with the lights on, so that you can see what you have to do. Then try with your eyes closed. Hold the film by the edges, as fingermarks will come out on the prints.

First, you need to cut off the film leader (the tapered end of the film), so that you have a straight edge. Always leave a short piece of film outside the cassette when you are unloading a film from your camera, if you plan to develop it yourself. Otherwise you will have to open the cassette with a tin opener or knife to find the end, and this has to be done in darkness. Take the film spiral out of the developing tank.

Turn the light off. Make sure the room is completely dark.

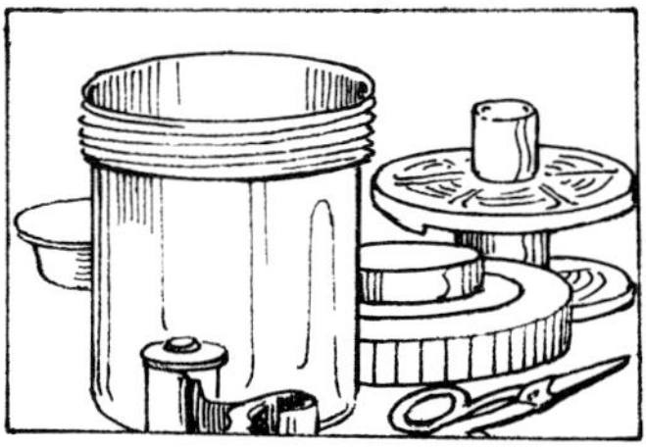

Have ready the tank, spiral and scissors

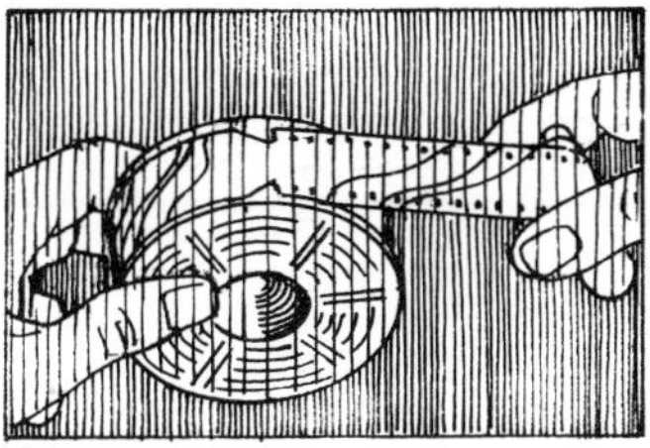

You must work in complete darkness

Holding the film with the cassette hanging downwards, feed the end of the film on to the spiral, under the guide points and on to the two ball bearings. Load the film by rotating the two halves of the reel backwards and forwards. When you reach the end, cut off the cassette.

Put the spiral into the developing tank and fix the spring clip in place, if there is one. Screw the lid on the tank.

You can now turn the light on.

4 Now is the time to check again that the prepared chemicals are at the right temperature, 20°C.

Leaving the lid on the tank, you are going to pour the chemicals one by one into the tank, through the hole in the lid.

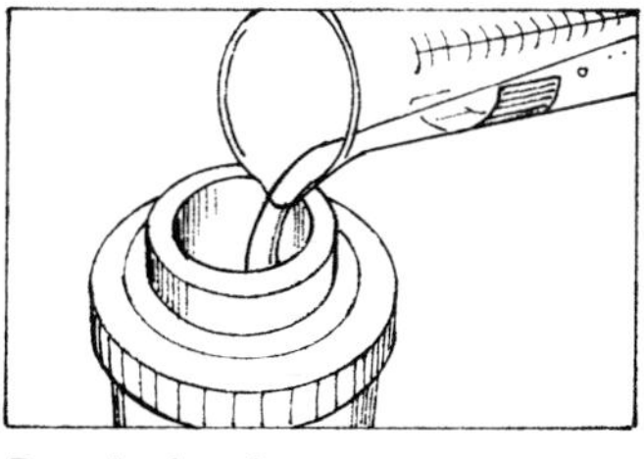

Pour in developer

Pour in the developer and start timing. Tap the base of the tank to get rid of any bubbles. Agitate the tank for 10 seconds, and then at intervals of one minute for the length of time the manufacturer specifies. (Agitate the tank by turning it gently upside-down and back again. Don't shake it. Agitation spreads the chemical evenly over the film.

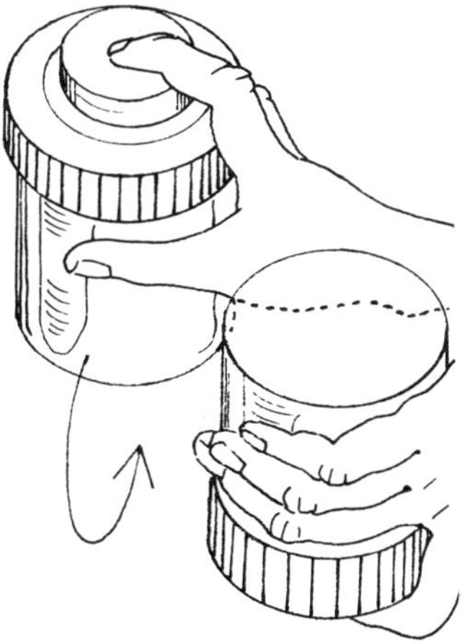

Agitate the tank

Too much agitation with developer makes the negatives dark.) Pour the developer into the waste bucket.

5 Pour the stop bath into the tank. Start timing. Agitate the tank for 10 seconds. You will probably need to leave the film in the stop bath for 1½ minutes (but check the manufacturer's instructions for the type you are using). Pour the stop bath back into the dark bottle for mixed stop bath, using a funnel.

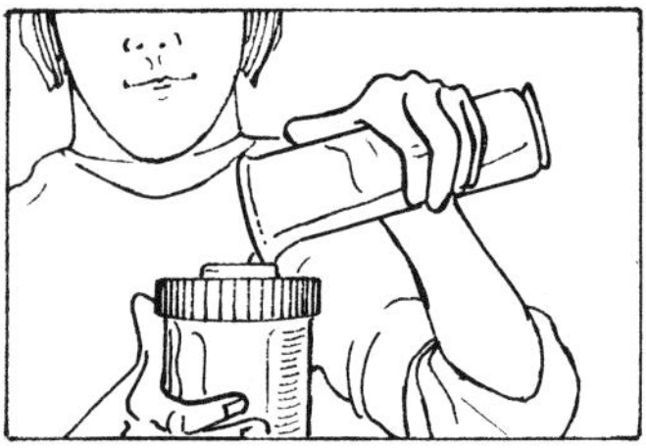

Pour fixer into tank

6 Pour the fixer into the tank. Start timing, and agitate for 10 seconds. Leave for about 3 minutes. (Check with the manufacturer's instructions.) You can then open the tank, because the light will not damage the film. Check that the end of the film looks clear. A 'milky' appearance means it is not quite ready, so replace the lid and fix for a minute or two longer. Use a dark bottle to keep mixed fixer.

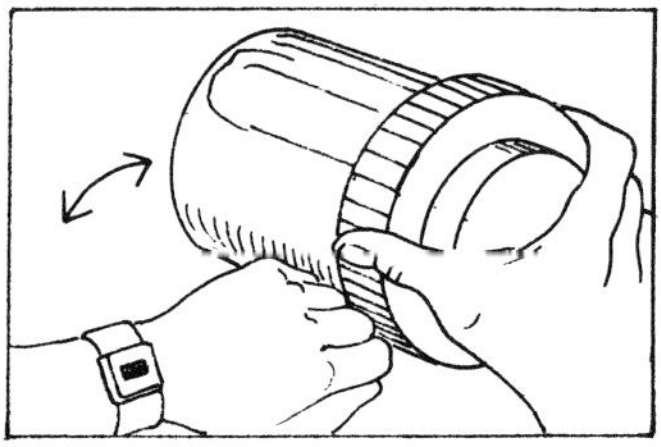

Time the fixer

7 Wash the film by running cold water into the tank. You could attach a rubber hose to the tap and put the other end into the top of the tank, or you could fill and empty the tank under the tap several times. You need to wash the film for at least 20 minutes if you are using a fixer with hardener (hardener prevents the negative getting scratched too easily). If you are using a fixer without hardener, the washing time is shorter. You can fill the tank with water, agitate 5 times, and empty it; refill, agitate 10 times, empty; refill, agitate 20 times, empty, and remove the film.

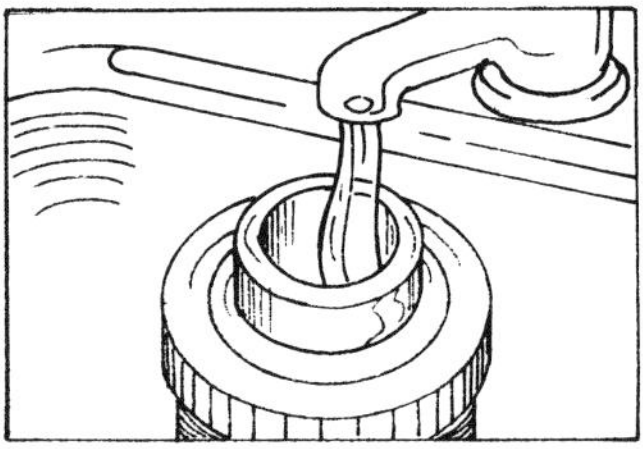

Wash the film

8 Take the spiral out of the tank, unload the film and hang it up to dry. You can set up a string clothes line to dry film, or hang each film from a nail in the wall. Use film clips or clothes pegs, putting one on each end so that the film hangs straight, and make sure there is no dust flying about as this will stick to the wet negatives.

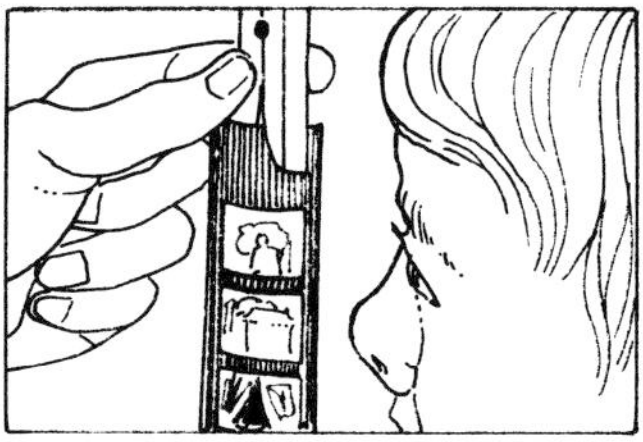

Use pegs to hang the film

9 Cut the dry negatives into strips of five or six frames and keep them in negative folders until you are ready to make your prints.

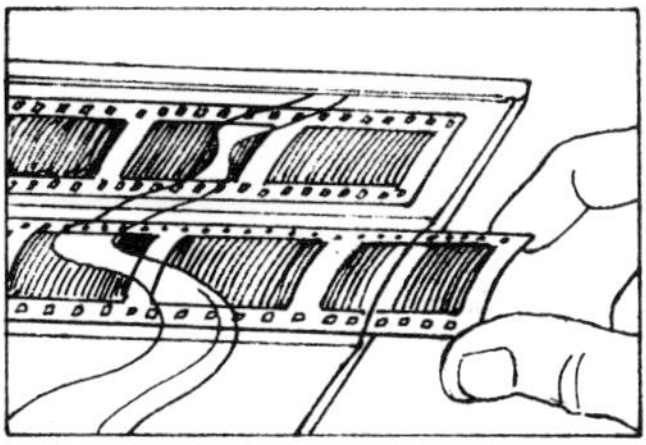

Keep negatives in holders

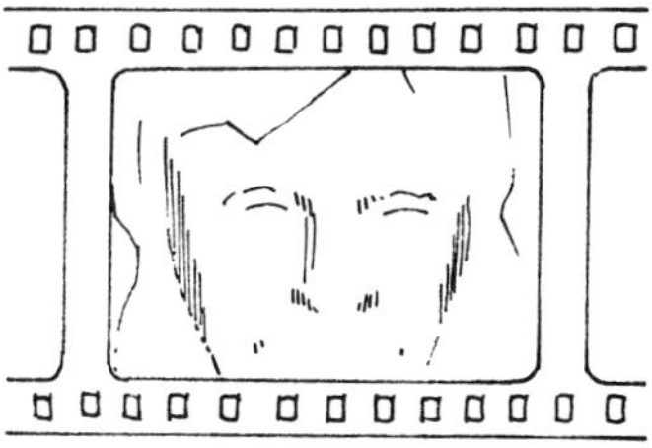

Thin negative

All the timings given should be checked against the instructions for the chemicals you are using. You will find that most manufacturers give clear instructions about dilution and the length of time film should be left in each solution. If you are in doubt, ask the photographic dealer for more details when you buy the chemicals.

What Went Wrong?

You will sometimes be disappointed when you look at your film and see that there is something wrong with the negatives. What has happened?

A negative is the opposite of a print (a positive). The shadow or dark areas are light on the negative, and the highlights or light bits are dark. A good negative should not be too thin or too dense, and should have detail in both the dark and the light parts. Here are some of the mistakes that can happen.

THIN NEGATIVES

If the image looks faint, with no dark parts, it could be that you under-exposed the negative in the camera, but if the whole film is the same, it probably means that it was not in the developer for long enough, or the developer was too cold.

DENSE NEGATIVES

If the negatives are too dark, this could mean over-exposure in the camera, or that the film was in the developer for too long, or the developer was too warm.

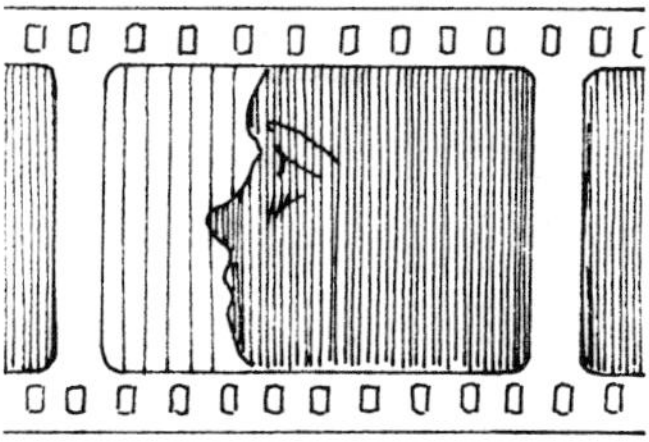

Dense negative

DOUBLE EXPOSURE ON ALL FRAMES

The film has been through the camera twice. If you are leaving the leader showing when you wind back the film, make sure that you keep exposed film in a separate place from new film.

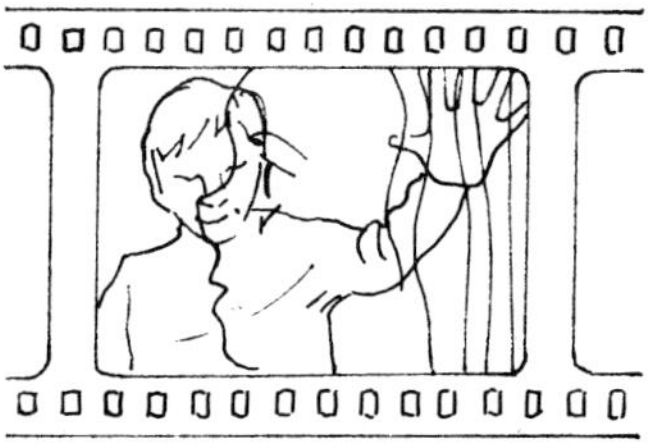

Double exposure

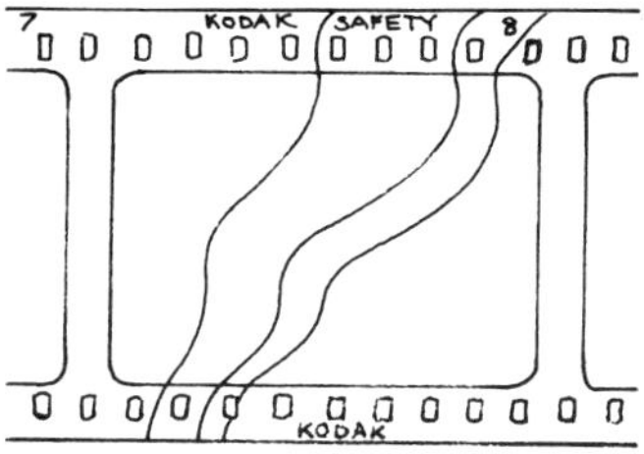

Clear film, except for film name

CLEAR FILM, EXCEPT FOR THE FILM NAME

If the film has no images, it hasn't been through the camera – you may have loaded it wrongly or there may be a fault in your camera.

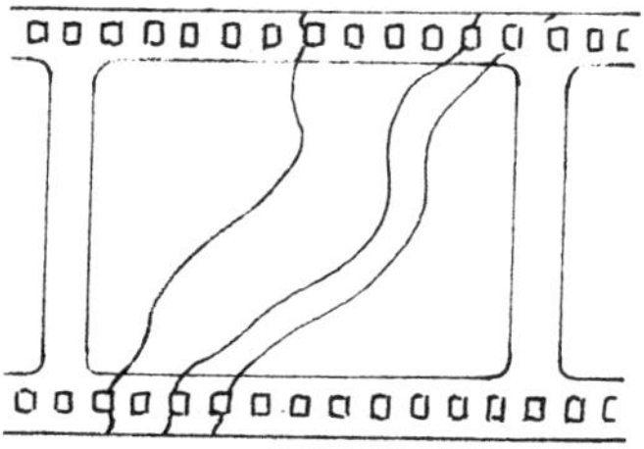

Completely clear film

CLEAR FILM, WITHOUT THE FILM NAME

If the film is completely clear, you muddled your chemicals and used the fixer before the developer.

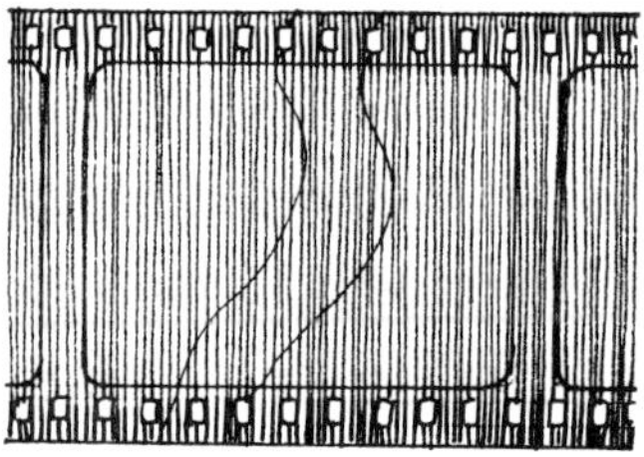

Black film

BLACK FILM

It has been exposed to the light (FOGGED) before or during development.

The film can also be spoilt by specks of dust, or by drying marks which show up as blotches on the negatives. You can sometimes wipe these off gently. If not, wash the film again.

CHAPTER 15

Making Black and White Prints

So now you have developed your black and white film and have several negatives to blow up into prints.

As well as the equipment described in the previous chapter, for developing films, you also need a certain amount of equipment for printing. Basically, for your wet area, you will need three trays or dishes for chemicals, and a fourth slightly larger tray for washing the prints. The three trays are for developer, stop and fix, and should always be used for the same chemical, so label them clearly. (It is easier if each tray is a different colour.) The trays should be made of plastic and be large enough to hold your printing paper without bending it. The washing tray should be large enough to hold several prints at a time, so that you can leave them in there until you have finished a session if you want to. You also need two pairs of PRINT TONGS for lifting the prints from one dish to another, because the chemicals should not come in contact with one another. (Keep one pair for developer and the other for stop and fixer.)

PHOTOGRAPHIC PAPER is a special light-sensitive paper. You can buy various types in different sizes. The paper can have a glossy or a matt finish: glossy is the most popular and it is best to start with this. It may be BROMIDE or RESIN-COATED. These names refer to the emulsions used for coating the paper – silver bromide or a plastic coating which does not absorb the chemicals. Bromide paper takes longer to use because it needs a lot of washing to remove the chemicals, which means that drying takes longer too. Resin-coated paper is easier, and does not curl so much.

Paper also comes in different grades, from hard to soft. The hard grades – 4 and 5 – give a print with a lot of contrast, and are good if you want a very black

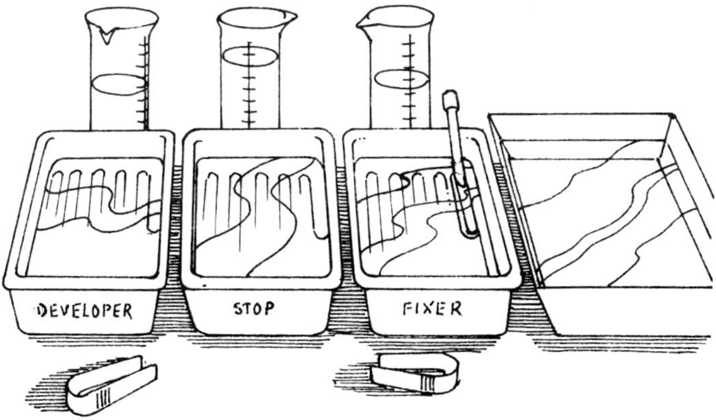

and white picture. The softest grades are 0 and 1, and these bring out subtle tones. Choose a middle grade – 2 or 3 – to start with and experiment with the others later. A good size for enlargements is 20 cm by 25 cm (8in by 10in).

Making Contact Prints

If you want to look at your pictures before you choose which to enlarge, you can make a sheet of CONTACT PRINTS. These are tiny prints of all the negatives on one sheet of printing paper, which are easier to look at than the negatives.

1 Make up trays of the three chemicals at a temperature of 20°C, according to the manufacturers' instructions for prints, and fill the fourth tray with water.

Switch off all lights except the safelight. (Because photographic paper is sensitive to light, you must use a safelight until the print has been fixed on the paper.)

2 If your enlarger has a red safety filter over the lens, you can take a piece of photographic paper out of the box and position it on the baseboard of the enlarger, shiny side up. Make sure the box of paper is closed. If your enlarger has no red safety filter, use a piece of ordinary paper the same size as the photographic paper at this stage.

3 Set the enlarger aperture to f/8 and switch on the enlarger light with the safety filter in position, if you have one. Move the head of the enlarger up and down until the light

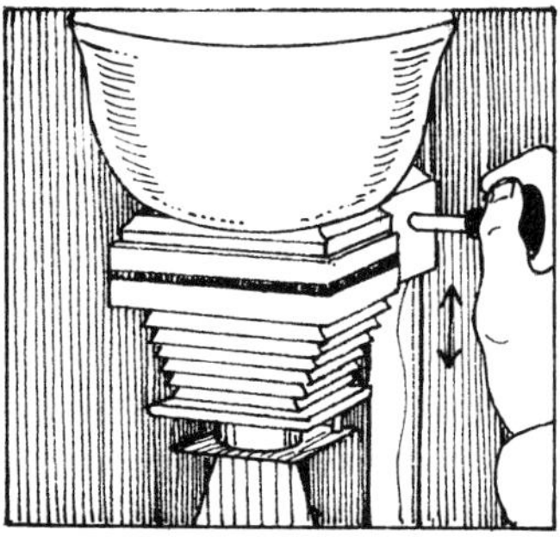

Move the enlarger up or down ...

completely covers the paper. If you have no safety filter, switch off the enlarger at this point, and change to photographic paper.

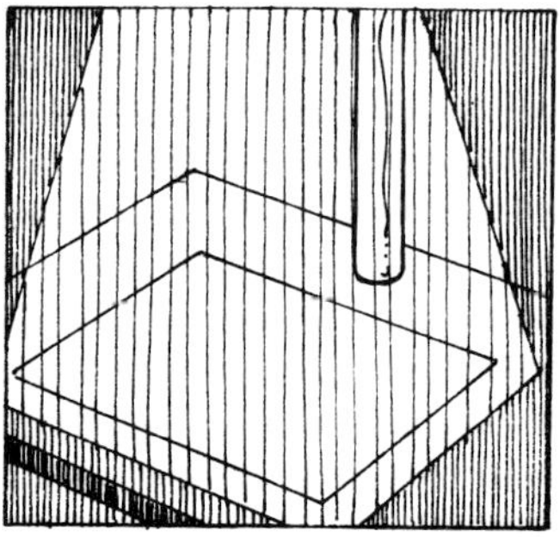

... until the light covers the paper

4 Place your negatives in strips of five or six, dull side down, on the photographic paper. Make a contact sandwich, by placing your sheet of glass on top of the negatives. Check that all the edges of the sandwich are square. Swing the red safety filter away from

the lens or switch on the enlarger, so that the light shines on the negatives. Try a seven or eight-second exposure. Then switch off the enlarger and process the contact sheet as with an ordinary print.

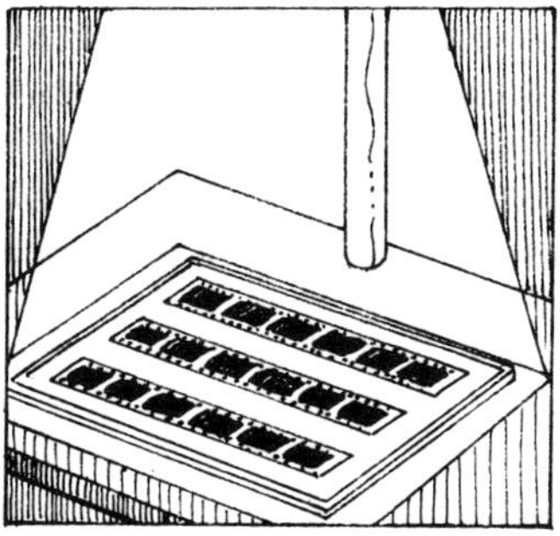

Place your negatives in strips of five or six

If the sheet comes out too dark to see the pictures, try again with a shorter exposure time. If it is much too light, try a longer exposure time.

Test Strips

The exposure time for prints can be difficult to judge, because it depends on the negative. For contact prints, you want a result that will allow you to see what the pictures are like, but for enlargements you need to choose the best exposure setting straight away.

From the contact sheet, you will be able to see if the negative you are going to print is too light or too dark at the setting you chose, and this will give you a clue, but it is a good idea to make a *test strip*. This saves wasting paper with trial-and-error methods. Some people make test strips for contact prints as well.

1 To make a test strip, you will need a piece of card for covering part of the negative. Choose one negative and position it in the negative carrier on your enlarger, shiny side up. Put a sheet of plain paper in the masking frame on the baseboard of the enlarger. Turn off the lights and switch on the safelight.

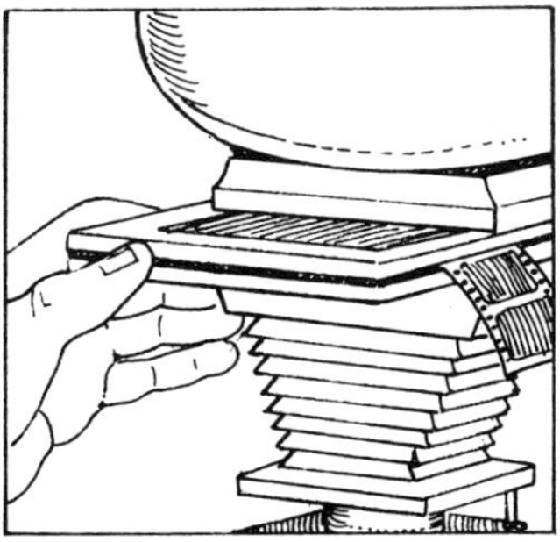

Position one negative in the negative carrier

2 Switch on the enlarger light. Adjust the height until you have the final size of print you want. Focus the image on the paper, using the focus finder if you have one, until it is completely sharp. (The enlarger is correctly focused when you can see the grain of the film through the focus finder.) Set the aperture at f/8 and turn the enlarger light off. Remove the plain paper and put down a sheet of photographic paper, shiny side up.

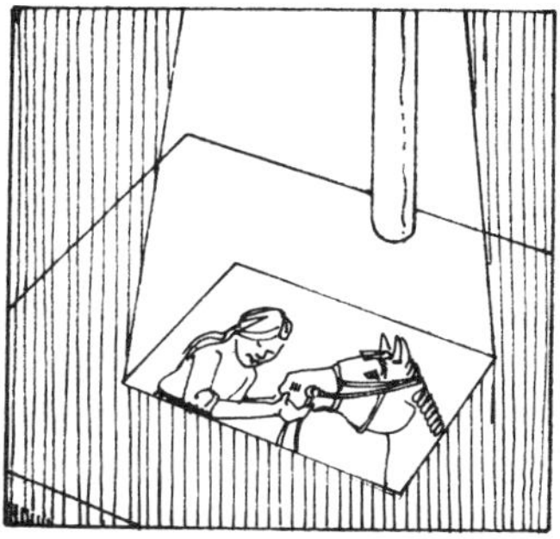

Expose sheet for 4 seconds

3 Switch on the enlarger and expose the whole sheet for the shortest time you want to try – say 4 seconds. Then cover up a section – one fifth if you want to try five different times – by holding the piece of card over it.

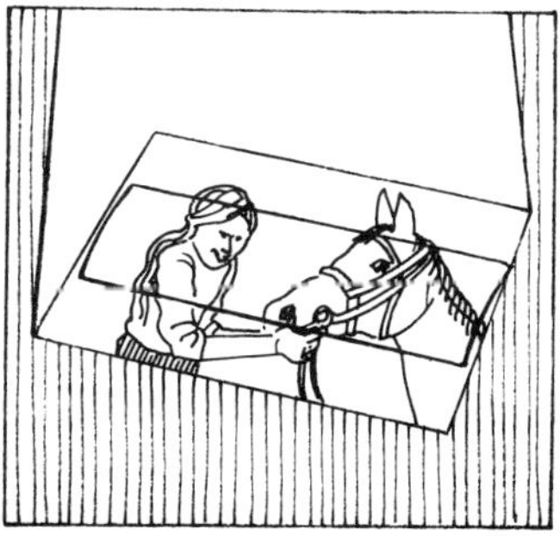

Cover a section with card

4 Expose the remaining sheet for 4 seconds. Carry on, covering up another one-fifth and exposing for 4 seconds more each time. When you have finished, process the test strip as for prints. You should have exposures of 4, 8, 12, 16 and 20 seconds, and from this you can judge which exposure time will be best for that particular negative.

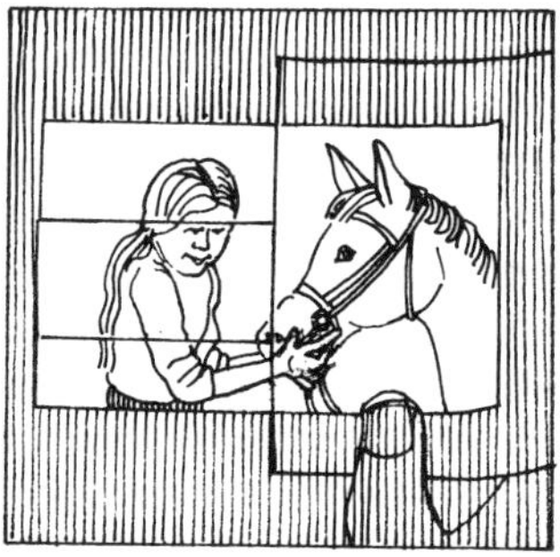

You can judge the best exposure time

Making a Print

Once you have chosen your negative from the contact prints and selected the best exposure from your test strip, you are ready to make a print.

You will need your three trays of chemicals and a water tray for washing the prints, the print tongs, a thermometer, the safelight, and the enlarger.

1 Put the negative of your choice, shiny side up, into the negative carrier on the enlarger. Set up the enlarger as explained earlier (see page 99). Switch off the lights and put on the safelight. Put a sheet of printing paper on the baseboard, shiny side up, and expose the negative for the chosen time with the aperture at f/8.

2 Still working by safelight, put the paper into the tray of developer, shiny side down.

After 20 seconds turn it over with one pair of tongs, and then leave it for 2 minutes, or the time recommended by the manufacturer, rocking the dish gently so that the developer is evenly distributed. Lift the paper with the tongs and hold it over the tray to let the developer drain off.

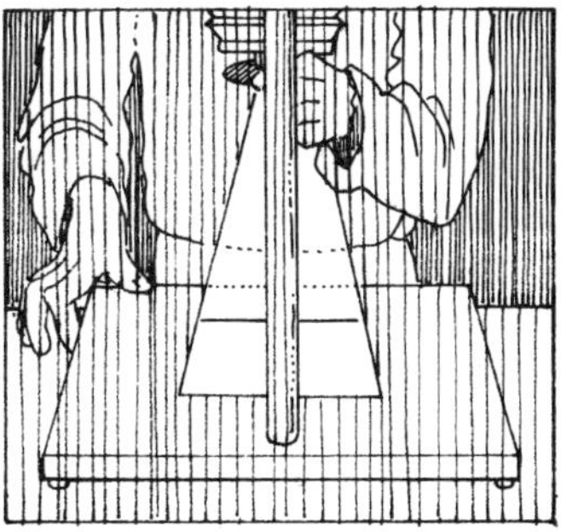

Expose the negative for the chosen time

3 Put the paper into the stop bath, again rocking gently, for 10 seconds.

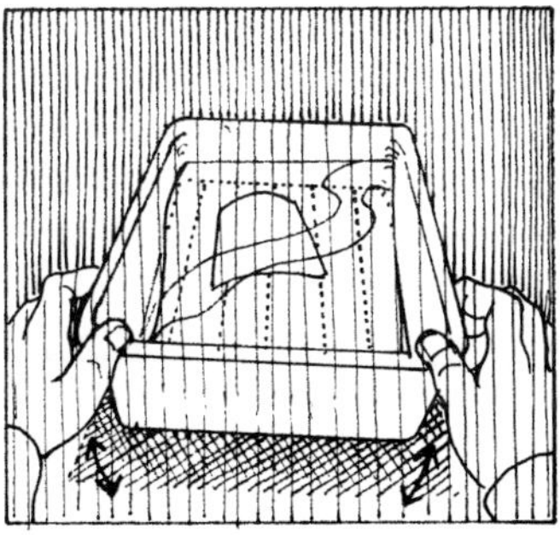

Rock the stop bath gently

4 Use the second pair of tongs to lift the paper out, let the chemicals drain off, and move

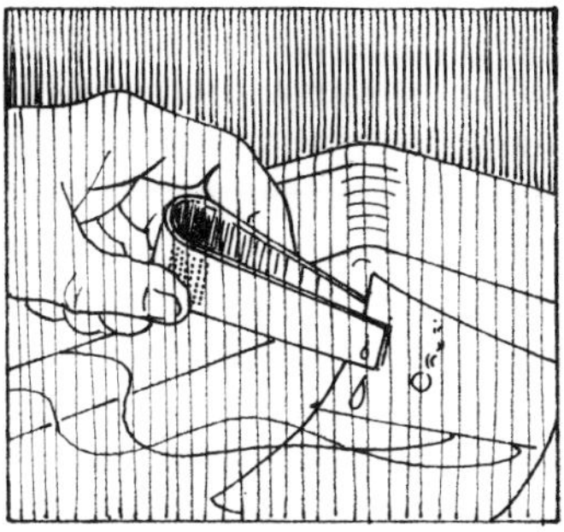

Use tongs to lift paper out

it into the fixer. Leave it in the fixer for at least 3 minutes, rocking the dish gently. (You can turn the lights on when the paper has been in the fixer for 2 minutes.) Then move the print over to the tray of water to wash it. Leave it there for about half an hour, then allow it to drain and sponge off drops of water.

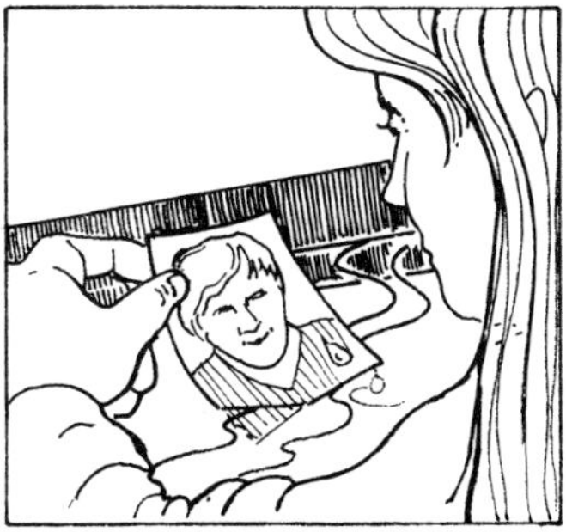

Wash the print

Improving a Print

Sometimes areas of a print are too dark or too light and you can improve these during exposure by techniques called BURNING IN and DODGING.

Burning in is used to darken very light areas that lack detail. Expose these areas for a few more seconds by shading the rest of the picture with your hands or a piece of card. If you use card, keep it moving, so that you don't get a harsh edge.

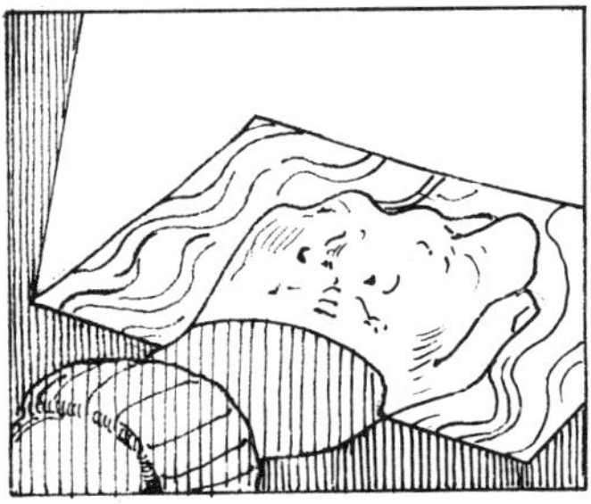

Use your hand as shade

Dodging is used to lighten dark shadow areas. In this case, you give shadow areas slightly less exposure. Towards the end of the exposure time, hold your hand or a small piece of card over areas that need dodging. If you use card, it should be roughly the size of the area to be dodged. Very small areas should be dodged with card mounted on

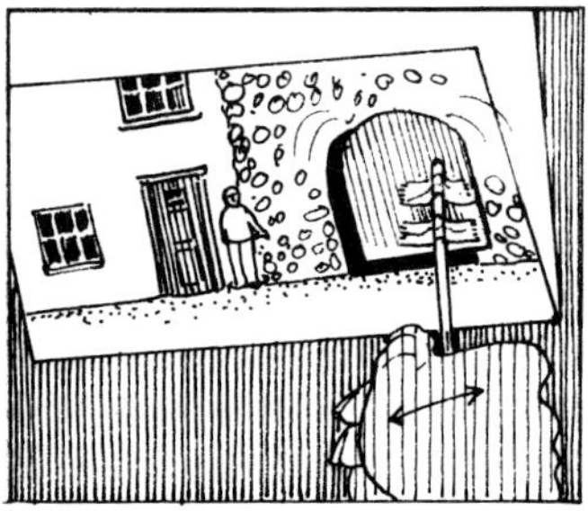

Use card mounted on wire

a piece of wire, so that your hand doesn't cover any of the print. Keep it moving to avoid a harsh edge.

When the print is finished, examine it for any blemishes, such as dust spots. These can be removed by SPOTTING. Spotting is done with a very fine paintbrush and retouching dye, or ordinary water-colour paints. Try to match the shade of the

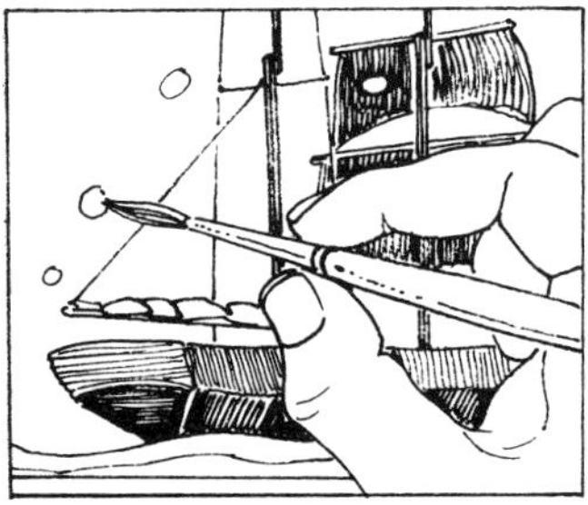

Spotting

area to be spotted, if it is not black or white. Dot the brush over the area rather than using strokes, which will show.

What went wrong?

Sometimes pictures do go wrong, and there are some common faults and mistakes people make. These can happen while you are taking the picture or while you are processing the film. We looked at some faults that show up at the negative stage on page 107. Here are some picture-taking mistakes that may not be noticed until the print stage.

BLURRED IMAGE

This is caused by camera shake or incorrect focusing. If part of the image is blurred and the rest is sharp, you have probably used too large an aperture for the depth of field required.

BLURRED MOVEMENT

The shutter speed was too slow.

HEADS CHOPPED OFF

The subject was too close to the edge of the frame.

DARK SHAPES IN THE PICTURE

Something got in the way! With a direct viewfinder, you may not notice that your finger, hair, or the strap of your camera case is in the way. Always check before you shoot.

PRINT LIGHT AND WASHED OUT

The film has been over-exposed.

PRINT TOO DARK

The film has been under-exposed.

WASHED-OUT SKIES

The contrast in the scene is too great. Next time, use a polarising filter to bring up the colour of the sky. Use a yellow or orange filter with black and white film.

SPOTS ON THE PRINT

Dust got in somewhere, either when you took the picture or when you processed the film. Keep your camera lens clean and brush off any dust before you take a picture. Make sure there is no dust flying around when you dry negatives.

Mounting a Print

When you produce a print that you are pleased with, you can mount it properly on card. You will need two sheets of white or coloured card at least 1½ mm thick, a cutting board, a ruler, a trimming scalpel, photo adhesive (in a spray can) and a glue stick.

Put your print on one of the sheets of card. Make sure there is room to leave a border of about 4 cm at the top and sides, and about 5 cm at the bottom. Spray the back of the print with photo adhesive. (Put it on a sheet of waste paper so that you don't spray the furniture as well!) Stick the print carefully on to the mounting card and draw the border all round. Carefully trim off the extra card.

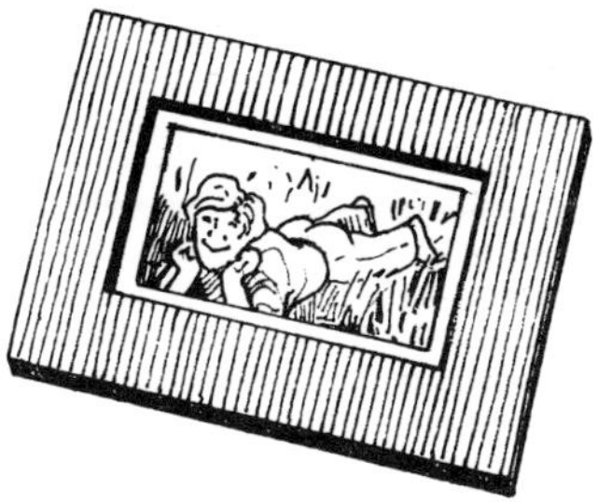

Mounting a print

Now cut the second piece of card the same size as the first mount. In the centre, cut out a piece the size of your print plus about 3 millimetres all round. This leaves you with a border to frame your print. Position the top mount carefully on the bottom mount and stick it on, using the glue stick. The effect is to leave a narrow border of the bottom mount showing all round the print. You can use contrasting colours if you prefer, such as brown or dark green with white.

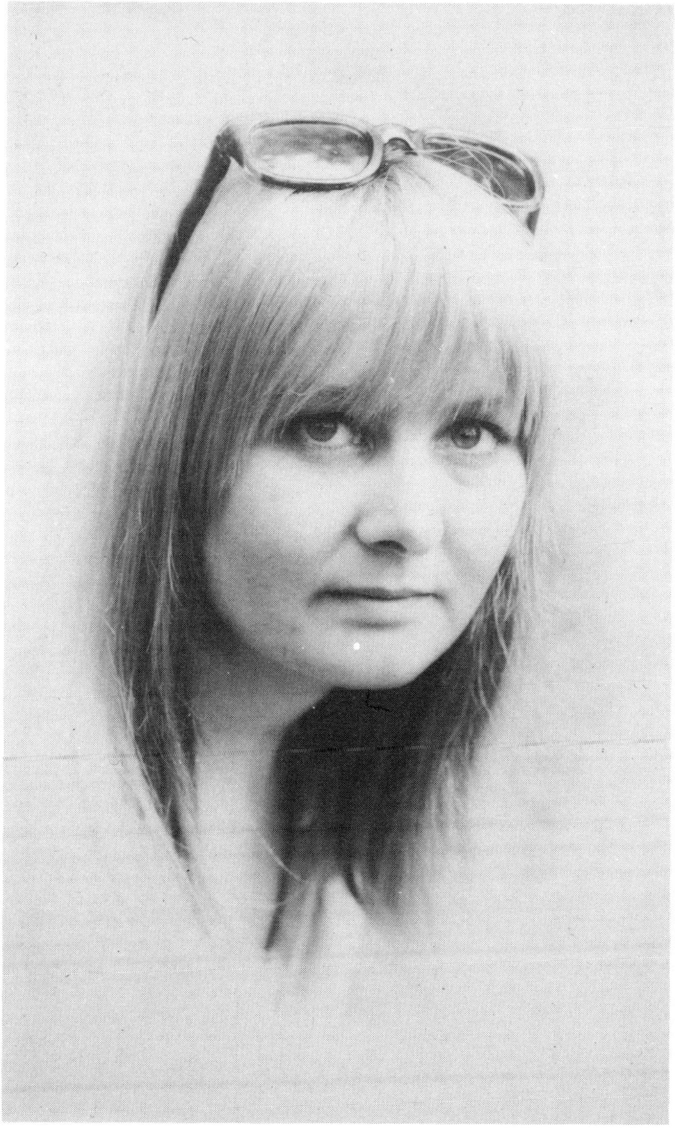

Example of a vignette

CHAPTER 16

Special-Effect Printing

There are several things you can do to make prints that are unusual. Some subjects can be treated in a special way, and you can have a lot of fun experimenting.

Sepia Toning

This is a very simple process which makes prints brown and white instead of black and white. It is suitable for any picture, but looks particularly effective on portraits. You could combine it with vignetting (see below).

Sepia toning is carried out in ordinary light. You can buy a kit which will tell you exactly what to do. You take a black and white print which has been processed in the normal way, and bleach it in a tray of solution supplied with the kit, to fade out the black and white image. The print then goes into a tray of the sepia toner, which brings the image back in browns and white. You can watch the image strengthening. Judge when the colours look about right (probably after about 45 seconds) and then take it out of the toner, wash it and dry it. That's all there is to it. You can also tone pictures in blue or red, using different kits.

Vignetting

Old-fashioned portraits were often presented as a vignette, which is an oval frame around the subject, cutting out most of the background. Choose which part of your negative to include in

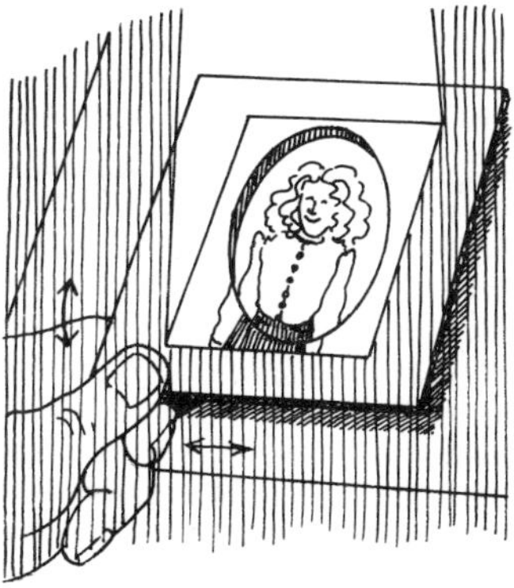

A vignette

the vignette and cut an oval to frame it, out of a piece of card. The card should be big enough to cover the rest of the picture. Hold the card between the enlarger lens and the paper during exposure. Keep it moving slightly, so that you don't get a hard edge.

Process the print in the normal way and sepia tone it if you want to.

Multiple Images

This is an effective way of using a single image, such as a tree. You print the same image several times on a sheet of paper, making a pattern.

By safelight only, sketch the pattern very lightly on the printing paper with a pencil before you start, so that you can see where to position the image each time. Take a piece of card twice as wide as your printing paper. At one side cut a hole in it the size and shape of the image. Hold the card with the hole over one of the marked shapes on the paper. Switch on the enlarger and expose the image. The rest of

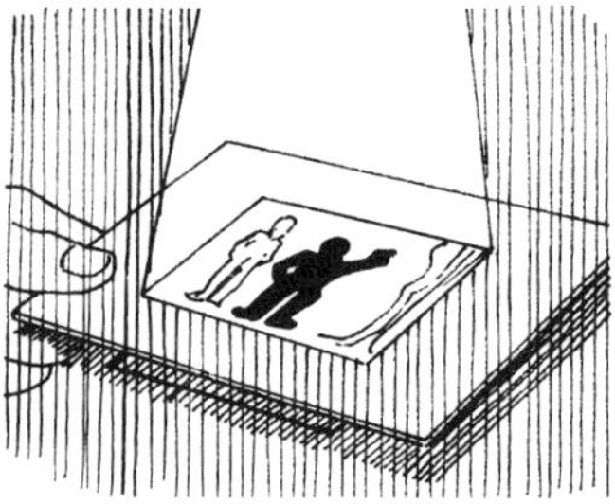

Making multiple images

the paper is masked by the card. Switch off the enlarger and move the card to the next position. Continue like this until you have completed the pattern. Then develop the print in the normal way.

Photograms

You don't need a negative to make photograms. You simply print the outline of objects by placing them on printing paper under the enlarger. When the

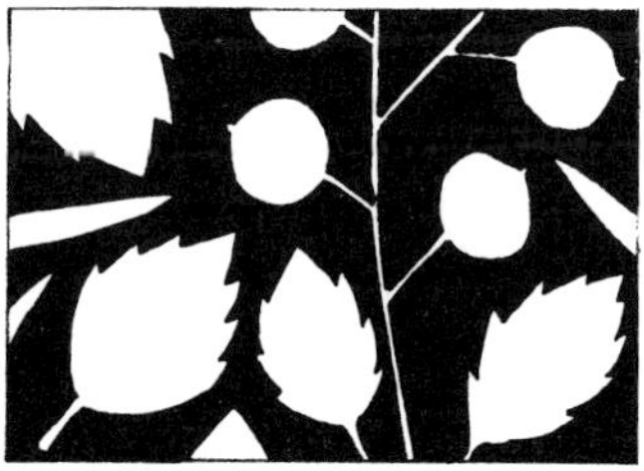

Photogram

light shines directly on to the shiny side of the paper, it turns black. The patches under the objects will stay white. Choose flat objects with interesting shapes and arrange them in a pattern. Process the paper in the same way as with a print.

Trick Photography

Sometimes you can get interesting or amusing effects when you take pictures. Photographs of people with trees or chimneys growing out of their heads shouldn't happen by accident, and they can look good if done on purpose.

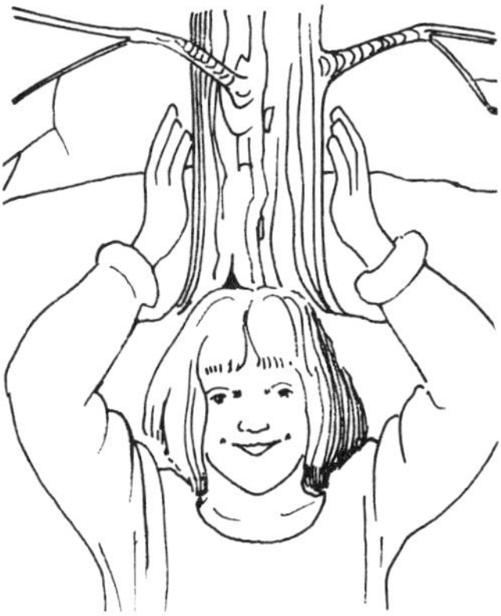

A trick photograph

You might like to experiment with this idea. If a person stands in the foreground of the picture, with a tree behind him some distance away, so that it looks small, the photograph will give the effect of a small tree at the same distance from the camera as the person. The person could have a suitable expression of surprise, resignation or shock on his face, so that the picture looks intentional. Line up the two subjects carefully and choose an aperture which gives you long depth of field so that both subjects are in focus.

Another trick along the same lines is to have a person holding up or pushing over a building. Use the same technique of

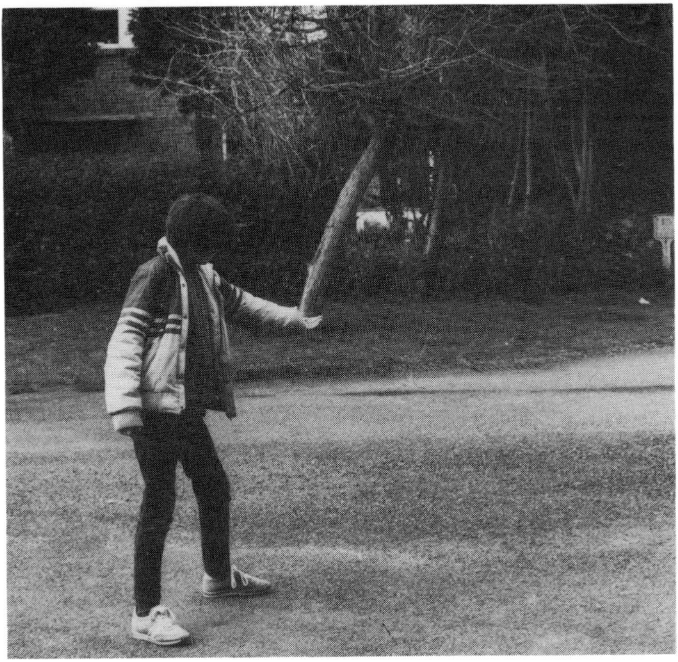

A practical example of trick photography

choosing a building some distance away from the person and line both subjects up carefully so that the person's hands look as though they are against the building. The person could even hold the building between finger and thumb or on the palm of his hand. Again, make sure the depth of field is long enough to cover both subjects.

If your camera allows you to take double exposures, you can have a lot of fun with this. A double exposure is two images on the same piece of film, and many cameras have a device to stop this happening accidentally because the film has not been wound on. Some cameras have a special control for double exposures.

Plan a double exposure carefully, so that everything is positioned exactly. Try to think

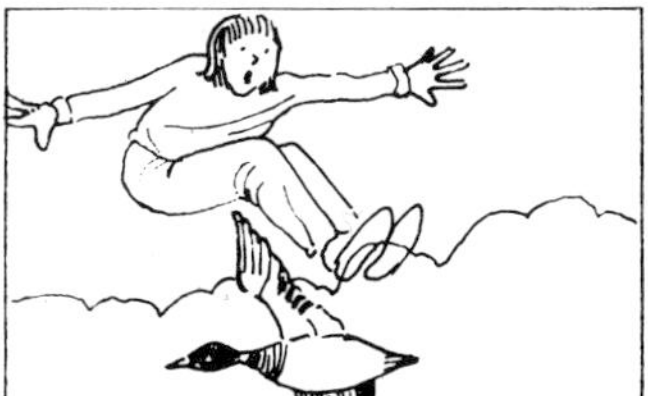

A double exposure gave this effect

up impossible situations, such as people flying through the air or a monkey looking in a shop window.

You can print two negatives at once to produce a double exposure. Put both negatives in the negative carrier and allow three times the normal exposure time.

Another way of creating the impossible is to cut out shapes and make them look as though they are flying through the air or climbing out of shoes or teapots. Stick cut-out shapes, such as witches or monsters, on a clean window. Position them so that

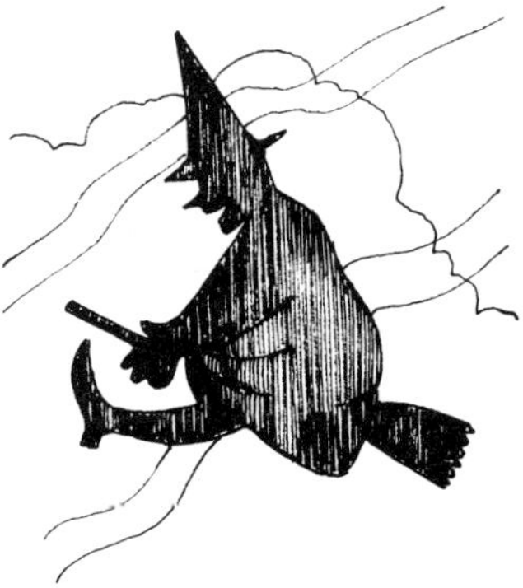

Use cut-out shapes to create surprising images

they are 'flying' above the horizon outside. Set the camera controls for the conditions outside and take the picture.

Cut pictures of people out of magazines and paste them on to card. Then choose an unlikely setting for the people, such as halfway out of a boot or a milk jug. Position the cut-outs and take your picture.

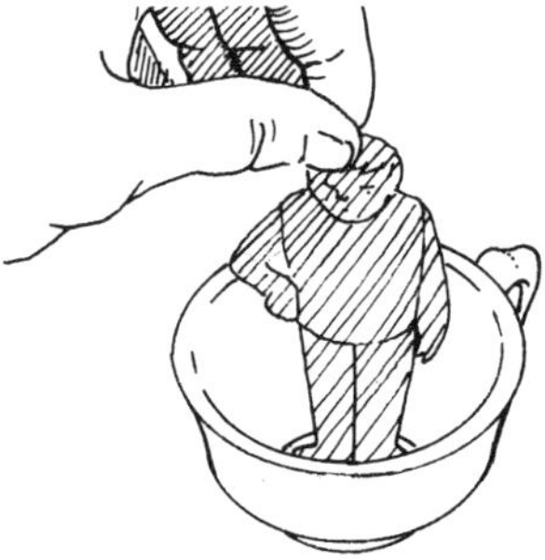

Photography can be a very exciting hobby, if you are always on the look-out for a good picture, and ready to experiment with your own ideas.

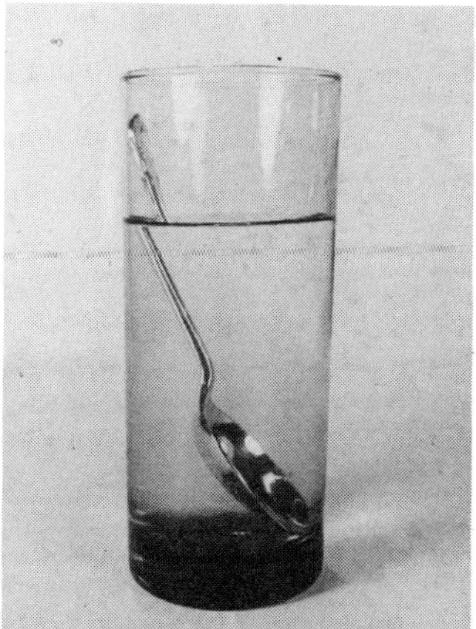

The water creates the illusion of the spoon being broken

Glossary

AGITATION

Method of moving the developing tank or tray so that chemicals are evenly distributed.

ANGLE OF VIEW

What you can see if you look straight ahead.

APERTURE

The hole in the lens which lets in light. The size of the aperture is controlled by settings known as f-numbers.

ASA

(American Standards Association) The most usual way of grading film speeds. The higher the ASA number, the faster the film.

BACKGROUND

Everything which is behind the subject of the picture.

'B' SETTING

A shutter speed setting which lets the photographer leave the shutter open for as long as the shutter release is pressed down.

BLOW UP

A process in printing whereby all or part of a picture can be enlarged.

BRACKETING EXPOSURES

Taking three pictures at different f-numbers to be sure of a good photograph.

BURNING IN

A processing technique for darkening light patches on a photograph, by giving a slightly longer exposure time under the enlarger.

CARTRIDGE

Film container used for 110 and 126 film. A cartridge is completely sealed.

CASSETTE

Film container used for 35 mm film. The film winds on to another spool in the camera and is wound back into the cassette after exposure.

CHANGING BAG

Lightproof bag for handling film outside a darkroom. A changing bag can be used to unravel film trapped in a camera, or to load exposed film into a developing tank.

CLOSE-UP LENS

Lens used for objects that are close to the camera.

COMPOSITION

The positions of objects in a picture.

CONTACT PRINTS

A sheet of small prints, the same size as the negatives.

CONTRAST

The differences between light and shadow in the picture.

CONVERTER

This changes the focal length of a standard lens.

DEPTH OF FIELD

The distance between the nearest and furthest points in a picture that are in focus.

DEVELOPER

A chemical used in processing to bring out the image on the film or printing paper.

DEVELOPING TANK

Light-tight container for developing film into negatives.

DIRECT VIEWFINDER

A viewfinder which is separate from the lens (non-reflex) and thus sees a picture from a slightly different angle.

DODGING

A processing technique for lightening dark parts of a picture by giving them slightly less exposure time under the enlarger.

EMULSION

Light-sensitive chemicals with which film and printing papers are coated.

ENLARGING

Making a print that is bigger than the negative.

EXTENSION TUBES (RINGS)

They are used to change the focal length for objects that are close to the camera.

EXPOSURE

Amount of light entering the lens to record an image on the film, governed by aperture and shutter speed. Exposure under the enlarger is the time for which the enlarger light shines on the printing paper to print the image.

F-NUMBER

Aperture settings are given in f-numbers on the camera. The higher the f-number, the smaller the aperture. Sometimes called f-stops.

FILM SPEED

The speed at which film reacts to light, normally measured in ASA. The higher numbers are the faster film speeds. These films react more quickly to light than slow films.

FILTER

Piece of glass or plastic which can be put over the lens to alter contrast or colour, or give a special effect.

FILTER FACTOR

The amount by which the exposure settings should be altered when using a filter.

FIXED-LENS CAMERA

A camera which has a standard lens only. The lens cannot be changed for one of a different focal length.

FIXER

Chemical used during processing, for fixing the image on the film or printing paper.

FLASH

Bright light used on the camera for taking pictures in dim light.

FOCAL LENGTH

Distance from the lens to the film when the lens is focused at infinity. Expressed in millimetres.

FOCAL POINT

The main theme of subject of the picture.

FOCUSING

Making an image sharp with the focusing control on the camera.

FOGGING

A film which is exposed to light in the camera or during processing, and is spoiled, is fogged.

FOREGROUND

Everything in front of the subject of the picture.

GRAIN

The dots that make up a photograph.

GUIDE NUMBERS

Numbers to use with flash to find the correct f-number to use.

INFINITY

A symbol on the camera, like a figure 8 on its side, which means that everything as far as the eye can see is in focus.

LENS

Circle of glass through which light passes into the camera. Different lenses can be used for different functions, for example, close-up or long-distance work.

LIGHT METER

Used for measuring the correct exposure needed for a particular picture. Can be part of the camera, or a separate hand-held meter.

NEGATIVE

The image on the film in which all the blacks are white and all the whites black. On colour film the colours are also reversed, though this is more complex.

NON-REFLEX CAMERAS

Cameras which have direct viewfinders (see reflex cameras).

OVER-EXPOSURE

Too much light has been allowed to reach the film, giving a dark negative and a pale print.

PANNING

Following a moving subject with the camera, to give the effect of a sharp subject and blurred background.

PARALLAX ERROR

A problem which arises with direct viewfinders. Because the lens sees a slightly different image, parts of the picture that are too near the edge of the frame may be lost.

RANGEFINDER

A focusing system sometimes found on non-reflex cameras, which shows a double image until correctly focused.

REFLEX CAMERA

Single lens reflex or twin lens reflex cameras have viewfinders connected to the lens by mirrors, so that the lens sees exactly the same image as the viewfinder.

SAFELIGHT

Red light for using in the darkroom. It will not spoil printing paper as white light will.

SHUTTER

Controls the light coming into the camera through the aperture. The shutter stays open for the length of time you have set on the shutter speed dial, measured in fractions of a second.

SILHOUETTE

An outline shape with no details visible.

STOP BATH

Chemical used during processing to stop the action of the developer.

TEST STRIP

Series of different exposure times given to the same print during enlargement. Used to find best exposure time for final print.

THROUGH THE LENS (TTL)

Built-in metering on reflex cameras, which measures the amount of light in a scene framed by the viewfinder and gives the correct exposure setting.

TONING

Changing the colour of a print with sepia, blue or red toner.

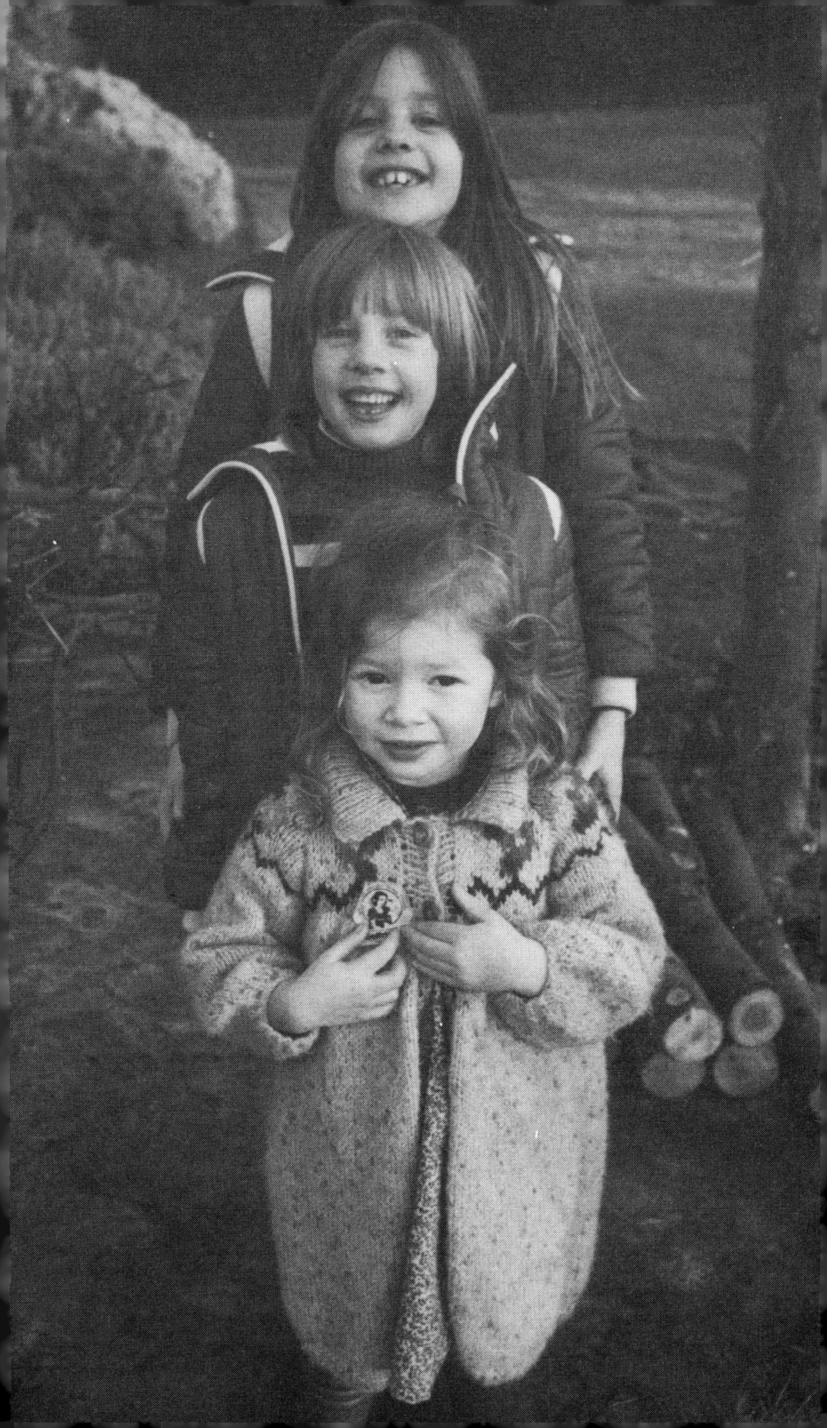

INDEX

Book List

Young Photographer's Handbook, G. Haines (Hamlyn)
Taking Photos, Lu Jeffrey (Piccolo Activity Fact Book)
Beginner's Guide to Cameras and Photography, Peter Hawksby and Jane Chisholm (Usborne)
Photography for Children, John M. Pickering (Batsford)
Taking Photos, John Vlitos, Whizz Kid Series (Macdonald)
Photography, R. Greenhill, M. Murray and J. Spence, Guideline Series (Macdonald)
Puffin Book of Photography, Christopher Wright (Puffin)
Taking Photographs, Colin Garratt (Ladybird)
Starting Photography, Michael Langford (Focal Press)
Photography – How To Take Better Pictures, Michael Busselle, (St. Michael/Artus Publishing)